FOR THE SAKE
OF HEAVINESS

FOR THE SAKE
OF HEAVINESS

THE HISTORY OF

by label founder and CEO
BRIAN SLAGEL
with Mark Eglinton

New York • Los Angeles • Nashville

FOR THE SAKE OF HEAVINESS:
THE HISTORY OF METAL BLADE RECORDS

Cover design by Randall Leddy
Metal Blade Records logo designed by Dan Fitzgerald and Brian Ames
Book production services by Adept Content Solutions

Library of Congress Cataloging-in-Publication Data available upon request.

ISBN: 9781947026001

Second Printing

Published by BMG
www.bmg.com

*For my mom, who gave me the support
to make my dreams come true.*

CONTENTS

FOREWORD

"If you form a band I'll give you a slot on the first *Metal Massacre* album, a compilation record I'm putting together for up-and-coming L.A. based metal bands."

And so it began. I was now officially on a mission…in the days where the whole musical universe centered around being signed to a record label, I had officially won the lottery. The way I spun it in my head, Brian Slagel had just given me a record deal. No ifs, ands or buts. Wait, the only thing missing now was having a band.

Rewind six months. The Country Club, Reseda, California, December 1980, a snot-nosed 16-year old Danish kid—fresh to the overly irrigated Southern California suburbs—walks around by his lonesome self, waiting for the Michael Schenker Group to take the stage, when he's approached by a couple of inquisitive fellas about whether he'd ever heard of a band from England called Saxon. "Yes, I have heard about Saxon!" I say matter-of-factly, somewhat puzzled by the question since I'm wearing a Saxon t-shirt in all its glory. And so the seeds are sown for a relationship that, thirty-six years later, hasn't really changed much. Brian Slagel and I, a couple of regular, somewhat disenfranchised kids—passionate music fans who have each in their own way embraced hard rock and heavy metal to make themselves feel part of something bigger, to each feel a sense of belonging—have now found each other.

When you tell the story of Brian Slagel and chart the course of Metal Blade Records, the three words that come to mind, at least to *my* mind, are loyalty, consistency, and dependability.

Metal Blade is the one label in the hard rock world that has always been at the forefront of the scene, rolled with the times, gone from triumph to triumph, been in the thick of the action,

outlived every single one of its competitors, and is revered and
respected by musicians, fans and industry peeps alike. And of
course, at the center of the Metal Blade universe is Brian Slagel.
Metal Blade and Brian Slagel go hand-in-hand. You don't write
the story of one without writing the story of the other. They are
inseparable. Since the early eighties when Brian and I started
hanging out, going to record stores and gigs, listening to music,
tape trading, corresponding with other like-minded metalheads
around the world, and generally being one hundred percent
enveloped in the DIY world of rock, Brian's passion, authenticity,
and dedication to all things metal has been unequal.

While my focus went in the direction of air-drumming, and
setting my sights on scraping together a band, Brian initially put
his energy and enthusiasm into starting a fanzine called the *New
Heavy Metal Revue.* He would write stories and share anecdotes of
his favorite bands, their treks through Southern California, review
recent record releases and gush on about the latest crazy, super
underground tapes that were King Shit until five minutes later when
the next band seemed cooler, more unique and more next-level.

One thing Brian was extra passionate about in the way early days
was the local L.A. scene. It soon became obvious that he was such a
proponent of all things Southern California that the aforementioned
Metal Massacre compilation was soon given birth to in his head. So in
the fall of 1981—after I had come back from my eye-opening and
life-changing trip following bands around Europe and was ready to
engage one James Hetfield in starting a band—Brian put together
the first of what would become a mind-boggling, endless array of
releases in the form of the premiere OG *Metal Massacre* album. It was
a classic chronicle, showcasing the best of what was happening on
the harder end of the scale around the Sunset Strip clubs and SoCal
in general. In addition, there was that earlier referenced, specially
held slot for his Danish snot-nosed buddy, who was in the middle of
luring his soon-to-be friend James into joining forces with him on the
promise of the record deal in his back pocket.

Metal Massacre became the gateway for Brian to enjoy and indulge his heartfelt passion. I don't know if anybody expected the attention that soon came his way, meaning that we were all so naive and busy "living it" that no one was even *thinking* of success at that time! It just fucking happened. And boy did it happen! In what seemed like no time at all, there were subsequent *Metal Massacre* releases and tons of cool bands signed like Slayer, Armored Saint, Bitch, Omen, and Lizzy Borden, among others, who were suddenly enjoying careers that they previously hadn't imagined possible.

Brian quickly developed a reputation for being that rare combination of authority and fan mixed with just the right combination of street smarts, and enough of a business sense to make it all function without ever losing its vital roots and his authenticity. In some ways, Brian was quickly becoming the American version of great British indie DIY labels like Rough Trade and Stiff Records, as well as their harder cousins such as Bronze and Neat Records. In retrospect, I'm certain he didn't know he had those qualities, and I'm sure a significant degree of the early success of the label was because of his subconscious ability to keep it a pure extension of his own personality, and to keep it real.

Every time I saw him in those early years, with Metal Blade further asserting its position in the rock world and wielding more and more clout, I swear he never changed one goddamn bit...still wearing the same cut-off t-shirts, probably the same sneakers as when I first met him, the same sweat on his brow, and the exact same excitement oozing out of him as he was describing his latest "find," just like years earlier in his Woodland Hills pad and its early primitive surroundings.

Here's the thing.

Brian is the true vanguard of heavy metal.

He loves it.

He supports it.

He really does live it.

He doesn't foghorn what he does or what he has done.

He just does it.

When you see Brian at a gig or a Kings hockey game, he doesn't trumpet what achievements Metal Blade have accomplished, because he isn't on this planet to do that. He goes to shows, bashes and events because he still loves it every inch as much as he did when he first grew the ginger hair on his youthful face!

You wanna hear what Brian's listening to, because *he* wants to hear what he's listening to! Do you understand? Brian isn't influenced by anyone other than his own ears and his own metal-plated heart. If it touches those places inside him, that's what counts. And in a world where everyone seems increasingly to be led by someone else—or other contrived, impure motivations—Brian continues to stand above and beyond everyone else in that regard.

That instinct, those qualities of his, are particularly dear to me, because let's face it, without Brian being Brian, and in his selfless way, casually mentioning to me that he would give my "band" (if I ever were to have one!) a slot on his first record, there's a better-than-good chance that Metallica would never have been heard. Would never been given its first break. There's a possibility James and I would never have become friends. Think about *that*; if Brian Slagel doesn't offer me a shot by giving my non-existent band an opportunity, then I probably don't connect again with James Hetfield. Wow! Let's not go any further...

So not only do I owe an immense amount of gratitude and appreciation to Brian for being Brian, for having the foresight and goodwill he has always had, but I believe the whole world of hard rock and heavy metal should tip its hat to him for remaining true to his core... for refusing to grow up, and for tirelessly continuing to champion the music, the bands, the vibe, the scene, the attitude, the pure *metalness* that Metal Blade Records have brought over the years, still brings today and, I'm sure, will continue to bring for years to come.....and hopefully outlive us all!!!

Lars Ulrich
March, 2017

INTRODUCTION

There's a lot to celebrate when it comes to heavy metal music. There's even more reason to do so when the most important independent record label in the genre reaches its thirty-fifth anniversary. This year, 2017, marks three-and-a-half decades that Metal Blade has been at the forefront of the scene.

Heavy metal music moves fast. Bands, subgenres, and record labels come and go—and the ways in which diehard fans consume the music are changing at a similarly rapid rate. But through it all, Metal Blade has adapted and rolled with every punch the business has thrown, releasing in excess of a thousand albums over these thirty-five years.

At the heart of the story is Metal Blade's founder and CEO, Brian Slagel. As you'll discover when you read this book, it was never his particular plan—as a young metal fan growing up in Los Angeles in the 1970s—to found a record label, or to even run a business. That just happened, and it was all driven by his unquenchable desire to not only hear the best heavy metal music in existence, but to make sure as many other people as possible heard it, too. It's appropriate that the story of how it all unfolded—the ups and the downs, from 1982 to the present day—should be told by him.

In addition, some of the key figures in Metal Blade Records' evolution are represented: staff, producers, fans, and—of course—the artists who have created the incredible music that has kept the Metal Blade world spinning. Whether they've recorded one album for the label or fifteen, they are all significant, because Metal Blade is and always will be a family.

Mark Eglinton

Chapter 1
MY METAL AWAKENING

I'm one of the few people in this business who was actually born and raised in California. I grew up in the Los Angeles area—in Woodland Hills—as the son of a single mom. By most standards, my upbringing wasn't in any way remarkable, but there's no denying that California in the 1970s was an idyllic place to live. The sun seemed to shine every day, which was great because I liked to play sports; I played baseball from the age of five. In many ways, I was just a normal kid living a very normal Southern California life.

It wasn't until I was eleven years old that I started to focus on music. Like so many people, there was a single, defining turning point and, for me, it was the moment my cousin played me an album by Deep Purple. It was called *Machine Head*, and when I heard it, I thought, "What the hell is this?"

Up to that point, I hadn't even thought much about music. Granted, my stepdad used to play some Johnny Cash and Jerry Reed, but he wasn't in the picture very long. Other than that, I had only ever heard what happened to be on the radio at the time, and in those just-before-the-explosion-of-FM days, that really wasn't much. Up until that moment, music was something that was just *there*. It was in the background. Nothing had hit me the way Deep Purple did on that fateful day.

Once I heard *Machine Head*, I immediately bought my own copy. I started feeling a powerful attachment to music—specifically *this kind* of music—that I had never previously experienced with *anything* else. It was as if a whole new world existed that was created just for me. It wasn't long afterward—probably just a week or

1

two—when my neighbor said, "Well, if you like Deep Purple, you should listen to some Black Sabbath." He played me *Sabbath Bloody Sabbath*, and life changed all over again.

And then I got lucky at the right time ...

FM radio was just starting to expand during late 1975 and early 1976. As part of that growth, a radio station popped up in LA called KWEST. Even then, they were routinely playing music by bands like UFO, Judas Priest, and KISS. They were one of the very first stations to start playing music of that kind at all. And I absorbed every bit of it.

Then I started going out and buying all these different albums, like UFO's *Force It*, Judas Priest's *Sad Wings of Destiny*, and *Dressed to Kill* by KISS. You could categorically say that I was totally hooked on the whole idea of heavy metal. I had embarked on a trip down a dark path, and I was only in junior high school.

Despite the new fascination, I was a good student. There was a really good reason for that; we didn't have much money in the family, but I remember my mom saying, "If you get straight A's, I'll buy you a stereo." Fueled by my growing metal obsession, I proceeded to get straight A's!

By the time I got to high school and could drive, I was able to go to a lot of live shows. Prior to that, I had stared at the show posters, desperately hoping to go, but never being able to. I was too young, didn't have anyone to go with, and, of course, was always getting resistance from my mom when I said things like, "Hey, can I go see Black Sabbath tonight?" She just said no, and that, I suppose, was understandable.

Once I had access to a car, I started going crazy. When I was eighteen, in 1979, I went to around 250 concerts in that year alone. I turned up at everything and anything that was going on in the Los Angeles area: club shows, bigger outdoor live concerts— literally anything—sometimes even to see bands that I didn't really particularly like. It didn't matter. The buzz I got from live music didn't discriminate.

There were a whole bunch of different scenes happening at once, so I was spoiled for choice. On the more punk-oriented side were bands like Dead Kennedys, X, Wall of Voodoo, and Oingo Boingo. On the more rock side of things was, of course, Van Halen (who were already starting to create a stir), Quiet Riot, and Snow (featuring Carlos Cavazo, who later joined Quiet Riot). But my favorite heavy band at the time was Xciter—the version that George Lynch played in. It seems like I went to see them a million times. They were my absolute go-to metal band for a long while.

At the other end of the spectrum was a new wave band I just loved called The Kats, fronted by a guy named Freddy Moore, who was married to Demi Moore long before she ever became an actress. I thought they were phenomenal. The Kats were selling out two shows per night at the Roxy or the Starwood.

I thought both my favorite bands would be huge, but neither of them found that kind of wider success. They just crashed and burned, and that really bothered me. I couldn't imagine how it was possible that they didn't break through in a big way.

When I thought about it objectively, I could see that, as great as these bands were, there was no real national scene for them to be part of at that moment. There was no MTV, and no promotion machine. Basically, these great bands were surviving in a vacuum in California. Seeing groups that were favorites of mine go nowhere left a lasting impression on me. Subconsciously, I stored that feeling of disappointment away.

Despite the differing fortunes of some of the bands in the area, I quickly immersed myself in all these disparate local scenes. It was then that the whole tape trading concept took off for me. Of course, I'd been aware of the idea that live tapes could be bought. A few years earlier, as a twelve-year-old subscriber to *Cash Box*, *Hit Parader*, and *Circus* magazines, I'd noticed all these ads for live tapes in the back of the various publications. I scraped together enough to buy one or two KISS and AC/DC recordings, but it frustrated me that I never had the money to buy everything I wanted. Now, a few years later, I had the means.

I started to think more along the lines of *trading* tapes on a semi-commercial level, as opposed to having to buy them, but that

meant I somehow needed to make recordings of my own to trade
with a growing community of like-minded people outside of LA.

I should say that I didn't really have any wider aspirations for
my life at that time. Because of the location of my home, I ended
up in a high school that was just outside the normal catchment.
The result was that I had very few friends there that I knew, and
that meant the whole high school experience wasn't particularly
enjoyable for me. You could say I did just enough to get through,
but that's all. My focus was on tape trading and going to concerts,
more than anything to do with school.

Gradually, I became a "regular" with some of the people who
were advertising tapes in the back of those magazines. In those
days, long before the internet, initial contact had to be made by
writing a letter and mailing it off, often to obscure parts of Europe.
Then you waited. There was no other way of making connections.
But when these people got to know you and the music you liked,
they'd expand your network by tipping you off: "Get in touch with
this guy. He might have some things you want."

There was a basic framework in place, but you had to be granted
access. It was like a secret club or fraternity. When letters came back,
that was the most exciting part of the day. When I was at school, I'd
look forward to getting home, hoping to see a full mailbox.

As a means of generating a larger catalogue of my own, I started
taking tape recorders to live concerts to make my own recordings to
trade. Granted, the quality at that time probably wasn't what you'd
get from a modern iPhone. But if you had a decent tape recorder
and gave some thought to where the best spot to stand was in each
venue, you could create some pretty decent-sounding concert tapes.
In fact, I regularly go back and listen to recordings I made back in
the late seventies, and most of them are still pretty good. You can
definitely hear what was going on.

In addition to making tapes to trade, I was also going to a lot
of record swap meets so I could sell tapes simply to generate
the money I needed to buy more music. The best known was
the Capitol Records Swap Meet, where, in 1978, people started

gathering in the parking lot adjacent to the Capitol Tower in Hollywood. There was no formal connection to the label; it was just a bunch of people selling records and, in those early days of collecting when no formal price guides existed, there wasn't much knowledge about the actual value of the records. There was so much stuff to find, and it was a great opportunity!

Very early in 1980, I got a package from one of my trader friends in Sweden containing a live AC/DC tape. At the very end of his letter he said, almost casually, "Hey, you should check out this new band from England called Iron Maiden. They've just put out a record called *The Soundhouse Tapes*. I've put the three songs off it at the end of your tape."

When I heard it, a familiar sensation washed over me. *What the hell is this?* I started freaking out. The music was so exciting. It sounded like the future. *My* future.

As crude as the recording was, this was the moment I became aware of a whole new phenomenon called The New Wave of British Heavy Metal (NWOBHM). I'd been a huge music fan, but I wouldn't have said that my tastes were exclusively metal. While KISS and AC/DC were my favorite bands, I still went to new wave shows, punk shows—all kinds of music. But discovering the NWOBHM was the turning point when I went from being a huge all-around music fan to being a total heavy metal guy. It was all over, and there was definitely no turning back.

I was hanging around various record stores in LA at the time— places like Licorice Pizza—and they always carried magazines from the UK, including *Sounds* and *NME*. Really, it was *Sounds* that started the whole concept of the NWOBHM. One of their writers, Geoff Barton, first mentioned the term in an article, and soon started writing about this whole new scene that was gathering a lot of momentum. I couldn't get enough of it, and I went full-on, hunting for every record by all these new bands that I could get my hands on.

A few months earlier, at one of the swap meets, I'd run into a guy named John Kornarens. We started talking, and it turned out John was a huge UFO fan. He was also into Scorpions and a whole bunch of other stuff that I was into. We became obsessed with NWOBHM together. It wouldn't be an exaggeration to say we were the only two guys in LA who even knew who any of these bands were. We started writing to the journalists in England for more information. Somehow we met Sylvie Simmons—the LA correspondent for *Sounds* magazine—and we became friends with her. We had instantly formed a vital link back to the NWOBHM.

John Kornarens

Sometime in the fall of 1980, I picked up a little 8x11 fanzine magazine, and in the back was an ad by this guy listing all these bootleg tapes for sale. It was Brian. He had everything from punk to LA bands, and then, all of a sudden, there was Judas Priest and Scorpions—exactly the kind of music I was looking for. I had already been getting tapes from other people—even at college, I had this girl who sat behind me who was a huge UFO fan. That was in 1979, and I was grabbing it from wherever I could. So, I called him and I went out to his mom's house first. That's how our friendship started. Then we'd go to the Capitol swap meet, which was a very vibrant scene at that time. It took place at night, under the lights, and you could pick up all kinds of European vinyl. Lots of the members of LA bands would show up to sell their singles. It was very cool.

Sometime in December of 1980, The Michael Schenker Group played a concert at the Country Club in Reseda. After the show, John Kornarens was walking to his car and, on the way to the parking lot, he saw a kid walking toward him wearing one of Saxon's European tour t-shirts.

Now, in 1980 Los Angeles, nobody even knew who Saxon was, much less had a tour t-shirt! Incredulous, John went running up to this guy like a man possessed. "You know about Saxon?" he asked breathlessly. "Where did you get that shirt?"

"Yeah, I just moved here from Denmark," the kid responded. "You know about bands like Saxon?"

"Absolutely," John nodded. "My friend Brian and I are *really* into this stuff."

As it turned out, the kid's name was Lars Ulrich. Whether it was the very next day, or a few days later at the most, Lars appeared at my house unannounced. I don't think I'd formally invited him; John had just told him where I lived. Lars had driven up in his mom's brown AMC Pacer from Newport Beach, where he lived with his parents. We spent hours talking about music and, as we did, it felt like another door had just opened.

It was typical for me and John to spend hours talking about the NWOBHM, but it really seemed like, until Lars appeared, nobody else in LA knew it existed or cared anything about it. It had always been difficult to actually get the records, which were only available as imports. We literally had to beg record stores like Moby Disc to order them under the proviso that we'd buy them immediately. Because I'd been hanging around these places for a couple of years, I knew people in the stores well enough to say, "I'll pay you whatever it takes."

Having Lars in our circle, this European kid on the ground in LA, made everything much easier—despite the fact that we all lived relatively far away from each other. He had come to the United States knowing absolutely nobody, and I remember him saying, "I can't believe the first two people I meet are two kids into exactly the same scene as I am."

Once every couple of weeks, we'd all pile into a car and make the record store circuit, looking for albums we wanted. The fact that there were three of us made it a little difficult, because we knew—if we were lucky—that a store might have one or *maybe* two copies of each record, but probably not three. So there was always this battle. We'd park the car, and then everyone would climb over each other to get out and literally *run* to the store. Lars was pretty good at that part. He would have already looked through five racks before we were even through the door.

By the time 1981 came around—and because one of my stronger suits in high school had been creative writing—I started thinking about creating a fanzine of some kind. I was aware of their existence in Europe, and had always thought the concept was cool.

It also occurred to me that nobody was doing anything similar in the US, so I suggested to John that we go for it. He agreed, and we created *The New Heavy Metal Revue.* I can't remember why we decided to spell "revue" how we did. I think we just thought it sounded a bit more cerebral.

John Kornarens
Brian said, "Hey, we should start our own magazine like Kerrang! *about LA stuff." I said, "I don't want to write it." He said, "Let's do it anyway." So we did. It was Brian's idea.*

Initially we just did record reviews and documented our thoughts about what was going on in the scene; the first edition was crude at best. It was all done on a typewriter, and I think we only managed to print a hundred copies. But things evolved thanks to our enthusiasm for the subject. Gradually, after we started calling every record company and anyone with any possible connection, we started getting a few interviews with the members of actual bands. I met a typesetter through a friend of mine, and I knew another guy whose dad ran a print shop. After a couple of issues, we had created something that looked somewhat legitimate.

To sell it, we basically went to every record store in LA and asked people I knew if they'd be kind enough to sell a couple of copies. Because they were all nice guys, they did it. Then I started looking in the back of magazines like *Circus* and using every conceivable connection I'd made in the tape trading world to get the word out. Again, people were surprisingly accommodating.

John Kornarens
Brian was working at Sears as an appliance salesman, I believe, and he was pretty good at getting people interested. We got advertisers and found people to write articles. Nobody was paid. Everything was done out of enthusiasm. That's certainly why I did it. I don't think the fanzine ever made any money.

It seemed like all this progress was happening quickly, but looking back, these endeavors took an incredible amount of time and effort compared to how easily similar things can be done today. It was so difficult just to get in touch with people! Letters took weeks to get responses, simply because we were championing a scene that was still at a geographical distance.

But, slowly and surely, a few pieces started falling into place. One of them was a standalone LA metal scene that was just starting to take shape. As a result, some good record stores were springing up around Southern California and, on a wider level, I gradually became aware of a few other people around the country who were starting to get into the whole idea of the NWOBHM. It didn't hurt that Iron Maiden was touring; Judas Priest was touring. It really felt like the metal scene was slowly emerging, and that made it easier to get magazines out there.

I remember, specifically, the first time I called Capitol Records about Iron Maiden. I said, "You have a band on your label called Iron Maiden." The guy on the end of the line just said, "Who?" Somehow I was able to finagle my way through to somebody in the press division of the company who *did* know something, and even that person said, "Wow, you really want to write about *this* band? Sure! What do you need?"

Capitol turned out to be very receptive to the idea, and the same applied to the management and labels of newer American bands like Manowar. At that time, there wasn't much going on in the way of promotional outlets, so the prevailing attitude was, "You're going to help promote our band? Sure! Why not?"

Because most of the labels and managers were in LA, I was pestering these people to no end with requests to interview bands or promote them with a feature in the fanzine. Of course, it was very much in their interest to be in touch with people like me; it was a symbiotic relationship in that I sold fanzines and developed the readership, while they got promotion for their fledgling artists. Everybody won, and it all helped to further fuel the embryonic metal scene.

One of the first interviews I ever conducted was in 1981. Iron Maiden was out touring the *Killers* record with Judas Priest and, for some reason, they weren't playing LA. Somehow—probably through one of my many calls to Capitol—I managed to get an interview with Steve Harris, but I had to fly down to Houston, where they were playing. I didn't think twice. I scratched up the money and boarded a plane. While Iron Maiden has been my favorite band for decades, the only time I have ever spoken to Steve Harris was in 1981, when I interviewed him in Houston.

By that time, I'd become a real record store rat. I'd be in the stores every day, sometimes twice a day, desperately looking through the bins for new stuff. I didn't exactly use a scientific method back then. I'd just look at an album cover and buy it if I thought it looked cool. I found out about Rush, for example, just by looking at the *Fly by Night* cover. I thought maybe it was a metal record! I had no idea. Back then you could buy albums pretty cheap, so I'd just pick up anything that looked like it might be promising.

There was one place in particular, called Oz Records, that was close to my house. It was a mom-and-pop store, really: part head shop, part record store. It was unique in that respect. Most of the others in the area, such as Licorice Pizza and Moby Disc, were part of a chain and only focused on records. My best friend at the time had a job at Oz. That was a dream-come-true for me. I'd be there every night until they closed; I'd stay there *after* they closed and, because of that, I started becoming friendly with the owner. Soon, for one reason or another, they ended up firing my best friend, and they asked me if I wanted to work there.

The first thought that went through my head was, "But they just fired my best friend!" It was awkward for maybe five seconds. Then I reminded myself that a job working in a record store was about the best thing I could possibly imagine doing.

I took the gig, and one of the first things I said to the owner was, "There's this huge scene happening in England called the New

Wave of British Heavy Metal. There are *tons* of records coming out. Could you give me a small budget to get some of this stuff in? I know I can sell it."

He knew absolutely nothing about metal. Not a clue. He was into seventies music, and the heaviest thing he was aware of might have been Jackson Browne. But he knew I was a nice kid, and a couple of the other guys who worked there encouraged him, too. He gave me a little budget, and I immediately called a distributor called Important, which was based in New York City.

I connected with a really nice woman there and told her what I wanted. She didn't know anything about any of it, either. I said, "I want stuff by this band called Iron Maiden."

She, like the guy at Capitol, said, "Who?"

I said, "They're really big in England. Get me whatever you can." And she did!

Because of the fanzine, I had gained maybe ten friends in the area who I knew could be relied on to buy pretty much anything. I quickly sold out the stock when the records arrived in the store. Then I asked the owner for a little more money and, over a pretty short span of time, Oz Records became *the* store for metal. People would drive from hours away because we were really the only place in LA that had a consistent throughput of NWOBHM material. In addition, I was hearing about new bands every day—acts like Mercyful Fate, Accept, and, of course, Motörhead.

Suddenly, I felt like I was at the forefront of something. I was a huge fan, but now I was driving the scene. One of the aspects of working in the store I most enjoyed was the opportunity to turn people on to new music. Metalheads would come in the door and say, "Hey, what do you have?"

Nothing would please me more than to be able to say, "Oh man, have you heard Mercyful Fate? It's amazing."

Having seen a couple of my favorite bands fail, I suppose there might have been a part of me that considered it a duty to promote great bands as much as I could. And now, with the fanzine and the job at Oz Records, I had the perfect platform.

It's important to say that, even when the NWOBHM music came back in the early eighties, metal was a genre that people outside of it didn't care much about. If they did know about it, they thought it was just a fad and that it would all fade away again. But I was the resistance. I thought it was the greatest music in the world, and I was willing to do anything I could to spread the message.

The next time I called Capitol Records, when Iron Maiden's *Killers* came out, instead of asking me who they were, Capitol bombarded me with as much Iron Maiden promo material as I could possibly use. We plastered all four walls and the ceiling of the store with posters, and I think we sold around three hundred copies of the record very quickly. Capitol was freaking out. The record store owner was really happy, too, because I was making him money.

※

One day a guy came into the store who I'd seen there a lot. He always bought a ton of stuff, but never really spoke much. On this occasion, he leaned across the counter and said, "You know there are some good heavy metal bands playing in LA, right?" It was David Carruth, the guitar player in a local metal band called Bitch. He told me about a few groups that were part of the scene—some of which I knew something about, and others I didn't. The conversation resulted in me showing up one night, sometime in 1981, when Mötley Crüe was playing on the same bill with Ratt at the Troubadour.

When people talk about the Sunset Strip scene of the 1980s, the first places they mention are usually the Whisky and Gazzarri's. But the whole LA scene started at the Troubadour. It was *the* place. It was a Wednesday night when I saw Mötley Crüe and Ratt, and the ticket was a dollar. This was back when those guys were pretty heavy, and obviously quite influenced by Judas Priest's image. The guys in Ratt were wearing black leather, playing Flying Vs, and Jake E. Lee was in the band at the time.

The show was great, and it opened my eyes. Before long, the fanzine wasn't just covering what was happening in Europe, but was also giving ink to what was going on in LA.

Chapter 2
METAL MASSACRE

In 1981 I was working on the fanzine, working every hour I could at Oz Records, and also trying to go to college. Like most twenty-year-olds, I didn't have any fixed ideas about what I wanted to do with a college degree. I suppose, in the back of my mind, I thought the journalism route might make the most sense, given everything else I was doing.

My getting to know *Sounds'* Sylvie Simmons, via John Kornarens, seemed like a helpful connection from a journalism standpoint. It also seemed logical to tell Sylvie about everything that was going on in the local metal scene. She was excited enough to say, "We should do an article about it for *Sounds*." We decided to build the whole article around Mötley Crüe, simply because they seemed to be the biggest band in the LA movement at that point.

John Kornarens

I had seen Mötley Crüe early on, and Brian had, too. I saw one of their first gigs at the Starwood. Then I saw them later at the Country Club, where they actually played a song that had me scratching my head saying, "I know this song!" They had done a cover version of a song by Herman Rarebell, the Scorpions' drummer. He had a solo album; most people don't even know that!

I had pictures, the single, a gig review, and the original press kit from their manager Alan Coffman. I gave it all to Sylvie. I was a doer, and when I think about it, I don't think that her true interest was heavy rock. So she relied on me to help her out. It was Mötley Crüe's first press in the UK.

The article exploded in the UK when it came out. *Sounds* was pleased enough with the response that they asked us to do a regular feature. It was basically a roundup of everything that was going on in the LA metal scene. Suddenly, having been these LA guys who were fanatical about the European metal scene, we'd become the voices of authority in a respected UK magazine for the whole movement that was happening on our own doorstep. It felt like we had every heavy metal base covered.

Around the same time, Mötley Crüe's two managers turned up one day at my house, where I still lived with my mom. They sat down on the couch. "We have 900 Mötley Crüe records that we've pressed," they told me. "What do we do with them?"

"Well, I know this distributor called Greenworld," I responded. "You should probably go talk to them." They took my suggestion and did a deal, and the rest is history. The album they made, *Too Fast for Love*, was the reason they didn't end up being on the first *Metal Massacre* compilation. In a sense, they were a step ahead of us. If I knew then what I know now, I might have responded differently. But at least I have one of the original 900 copies to show for it!

John Kornarens

Sylvie recruited us to go and scope out some of these LA rock bands that were up and coming, give a synopsis, and gather photos and tapes. She basically allowed us to give our opinion, and then she just wrote it down and it was published in Sounds *and later in* Kerrang!

While I took some accounting and business courses, I was doing none of these things with any particular business mindset. I just loved the music so much that everything else was incidental. But, living in Woodland Hills, which was a little bit out of town, I saw an opening. "Wouldn't it be so cool if there were gigs right by my house?" I remember thinking at one point. The solution? Become a small-time gig promoter.

Conveniently, there was a tiny live music venue near my house called The Valley West Supper Club. It was in an unremarkable strip mall, but somehow the booking guy there had brought in a couple of local heavy metal bands one night. I went to the show and met the promoter. "Hey, I've got this fanzine," I told him. "And I work in a record store. Maybe there's a way you could give me a slot once a week, and I could do a metal night?"

He was into it. "Yeah, sure," he nodded. "No problem."

It's funny that I thought I needed anything else to take up my time between the fanzine, the record store job, and my classes, but suddenly I was jumping into promotion, too.

At almost exactly the same time, I got a call from a guy at the local radio station, KMET. I can only guess that I'd become known as the main metal guy in LA, so he asked me if I'd be able to give him records to play on their new Sunday night metal show. I started a great relationship with them, helping them program their new show with material I could access through Oz Records.

I never really stopped to think about it, but you could say I was the driving force behind heavy metal in LA in that era. At the time, it didn't feel like that. It all seemed so underground, and the various ventures I got into just seemed like another way to fight for exposure for the music I loved.

The promotional metal nights started selling out every time I put one on. It even led to me promoting bigger shows at a couple of venues in Hollywood, and at the Country Club in Reseda. It was fun, and it was useful for boosting local bands, but it wasn't always enjoyable to have to deal with the money end—that part of the business where you negotiate with bands about how much they're paid.

Really, when I think about it, my motivation for promoting was at least a little selfish. Back in those days, people would, of course, enjoy some adult beverages and then get in their car. Having bands that I loved playing down the street from my house made more sense. I could drink without having to get in a car to drive across town!

I was still living with my mother at the time and doing the fanzine out of her garage. Because she worked as a registered nurse at a local hospital, mostly on the graveyard shift, we were usually like ships passing in the night. I saw her for maybe an hour or two each evening before she went to work at eleven and, as far as she was concerned, as long as I was getting good grades at school and wasn't doing anything too crazy, she was fine.

But, strangely, I recall always feeling nervous about what she thought about what I was doing. I wanted to just sit tight and see where all the various ventures I was involved in might take me. What was important to her at that time was that I seemed happy, so unless that changed, her attitude was very much, "All right, go ahead and do whatever you're doing." On reflection, I'm lucky to have had a mother who was so cool about this unconventional life I was living.

I remember getting a long distance phone call from Lars Ulrich sometime in the summer of 1981.

"You'll never believe this. I'm hanging out with Diamond Head!"

"Dude, you've got to be kidding. There's no way."

"No, no really I am…"

I was with John Kornarens at the time, and we were both freaking out. We couldn't believe that we were stuck in LA while he was over there, living the European dream life for the summer, hanging out with Diamond Head, Motörhead, and all these other amazing bands. It was all so typical of Lars. Even as a teenager, he seemed to have an uncanny ability to make things happen.

When he came back, he couldn't wait to tell us more about it, so he invited us down to his house in Newport Beach. While we were hanging out in his room, I noticed that he had a drum set in the corner closet. It wasn't even assembled; it was just bits and pieces.

"Why do you have a drum set here, dude?" I asked.

"I'm going to start a band," he responded matter-of-factly.

All I thought at the time was, "Sure you are, Lars…"

Even at that point, there was still a lot of frustration attached to trying to get the word out about a metal scene that nobody seemed to care about. If I put a band in my *New Heavy Metal Revue* fanzine in an attempt to generate interest, there were probably less than a thousand copies, at most, getting made, so the scope of the coverage wasn't particularly wide.

Then a idea came to me. Influenced by the overtly do-it-yourself attitude that went along with the New Wave of British Heavy Metal—where compilations like *Metal for Muthas* had started appearing in 1980—I thought, "Why don't I put together a compilation record of my own?"

John Kornarens

Six issues into the fanzine, Brian goes, "Hey, why don't we do an album like Metal for Muthas*?" And that was the start of* Metal Massacre. *At that time, I was still in college and working in the produce department of a supermarket to make money.*

I had no idea what the next steps should be; there was no handbook out there about how to release records. With a bit of forethought, I decided that the first, and most logical, people to contact might be the various importers from whom I was ordering stock for Oz Records. There were very few independent distributors around. One was Greenworld in LA—the guys I sent Mötley Crüe to—and the other was Important in New York, which would eventually become Red Distribution. I asked them both the million-dollar question: "If I put together a compilation album of all the up-and-coming metal bands in LA, would you guys distribute it for me?"

"Sure!" was the answer from both of them, so now I had no choice but to go and start talking to the bands. The slight problem I had at that point was that I really had no money—and that certainly was an issue given that it was going to be my responsibility to come up with enough cash to press perhaps 2,500 albums. Nobody else was going to pay it. Granted, I had some money saved from a very brief, part-time stint working at Sears selling appliances on commission, but not nearly enough to have any of the bands record anything on my dime. The only option I had was to go to them and say, "If you could record something, I'm thinking about putting this compilation record together. I'll get you on it."

Luckily, most of the bands already had something recorded and were totally into the idea. And those that didn't were willing to scrape up whatever small amount of cash they could to go into a studio. It made sense for all of us. I needed them to be on the record; they needed to be on an album because, back then, being on an album of any kind was a really big deal. Nobody was putting out albums, and there were no independent labels of any kind other than those that were still releasing punk.

After a few meetings and conversations where I enthusiastically pitched the compilation, the band Bitch, fronted by Betsy Weiss, agreed to participate. Cirith Ungol, a band from Ventura that had been around since the early seventies, said OK, too. Originally, Mötley Crüe was going to be on it, but they dropped out at the last minute, having been signed to a label following the article that John and I had published about them in the UK. Ratt was in. Malice was in. John Kornarens' sister was in a band called Avatar, and they ended up on the record, too. There was no shortage of interest. Pretty soon, I had the basis for a pretty good compilation record.

In retrospect, the location of Oz Records was key at that stage, too. Its spot in Woodland Hills was affluent enough, but it was also close to the mouth of Topanga Canyon, so there were two ways to get to the store: from the beach side, or from the city. Consequently, given that this was Topanga in the eighties, we had a bunch of rock stars living nearby who'd come in regularly.

Kevin Cronin from REO Speedwagon came in; Frank Zappa lived literally four blocks away, and he occasionally appeared. A couple of guys who had played in Zappa's band—and this was the *Joe's Garage* era—came in. The singer, Ike Willis, and another guy named Rick Gerard—who'd played bass with Zappa at some time or another and was friends with Oz Records' owner—were there periodically. As it turned out, Rick wanted to go into the studio and record something for the record. That group became Demon Flight.

Toward the end of the process of assembling the bands for the record, Lars, having been back from Europe for several months, called me up and said, "Hey, I heard you're doing a compilation. If I put together a band, can I be on it?" Not really knowing that he was actually going to do it, I said, "Yeah, sure!"

The backstory—and it has been written about many times already—is that Lars and James Hetfield had met and had been rehearsing a little, but couldn't, at the outset, find anyone to be in their band. Apparently nobody else had their knowledge of the NWOBHM or was into anything they were. So they couldn't gig— couldn't do anything. Nothing was happening for them, so when the opportunity to be on an album came up, they were going to take it. In fact, they were the last band to sign on to what would be called *Metal Massacre*.

John Kornarens

Around this time, Lars actually asked me if I wanted to join Metallica. He said, "We'll rehearse five nights a week in Downey." I already knew James and felt that, while he was motivated by Lars's musical knowledge, on a personal level he bonded with me more because we shared that Southern California ethos of muscle cars and Ted Nugent!

But joining Metallica meant I'd have to quit my job. My mom would have probably kicked me out of the house, and I was a month-and-a-half away from graduating college. I'd been told that if I didn't go to college, I'd get kicked out permanently. So Lars makes the call and says, "I'm putting this band together with James—you want to play rhythm guitar? James is struggling between playing guitar and singing."

I thought about it for thirty seconds. I was making thirteen dollars an hour at the supermarket, which was good money back then. I was about to finish college, so I said, "Thanks Lars, but I better not."

He said, "OK, no problem!" I had absolutely no sense that they'd ever make it.

A month prior, Brian and I had gone down to Lars's place, and he showed us this drum kit he had in a closet in his bedroom. He told us he was starting a band. I thought, "This guy's nuts. He's living in a townhouse in Newport Beach; everyone's going to kick him out because of the noise." He had this ridiculously humungous silver drum set. I just closed the closet door, walked out of the room, and said, "All right Lars, go for it."

John Kornarens and I had scraped together just enough money from here, there, and everywhere to get the compilation done. When it got down to the final days—when I had nearly all the tapes from all the bands together, and was almost ready to do the pressing—I still hadn't gotten a tape from Lars. Desperate, I called him and said, "Dude, we're coming up on the deadline here. I need this."

Nothing happened.

At the very last moment of the last day when John and I were mastering the record with the engineer at the Hollywood Bijou Studio, Lars came running up the street with his tape. They'd seemingly produced it the night before on a small four-channel machine on which you could just barely make a somewhat medieval recording. They'd recorded the track "Hit the Lights" and, on the original pass, James played the guitars, the bass and sang; Lars played drums, and Lloyd Grant, another one of Lars's friends, played the lead. That was the original version.

Lars brought the recording in on a cassette. To properly master something like that it, had to be bumped up to a reel-to-reel. Luckily, one of the guys who worked at the record store had given us a crazy good deal to use the studio, but there was still an additional fifty-dollar charge to transfer the tape.

I didn't have fifty bucks; Lars certainly didn't have fifty bucks. Thankfully, John Kornarens did, so we were able to put the Metallica song on the record. Otherwise, I'm not sure what the hell would have happened there!

I was already pulling a million favors to assemble this compilation record. I couldn't possibly focus on every detail all the time. I just wanted it to exist. The girl who agreed to do all the typesetting—who also did the typesetting for the fanzine—was doing everything for free. And in those days, somebody had to sit and laboriously put the letter block together in preparation for the actual printing process.

Lars had literally given me everything at the last minute: the name of the band, the song, and everything else. When I gave it all to the typesetter—and because the word *Metallica* didn't exist in the English language at that time—she somehow felt that the word should be spelled in a different way. It was so desperately late; I had no reference from which to approve it, so we just went with it. After the record went to press, I looked at the back of it, and my heart sank. It was spelled "Mettallica." At that point, there was nothing whatsoever I could do about it. It was one of many rookie errors I'd make.

Interestingly, as an aside, the guy who did the actual printing for me also did some work for the LA Kings and the Lakers. Instead of paying him, they just gave him tickets for games. He wasn't a hockey fan, but knew that I was. He said, "Hey, do you want these Kings season tickets?" I started going to games and became completely obsessed with hockey. That has continued until today. It's my therapy. At one point, I was going to over a hundred hockey games per year.

Though I wasn't doing any of this with a view to starting a record label, I still felt that I had to come up with an actual name for the label on which this compilation project was going to be released. I originally wanted to call it Skull and Crossbones Records. But, from memory, I think one of the guys from Blondie had just started his own independent label under that exact name. I was really bummed out, thinking, "What are we going to call this thing now?"

I then decided I definitely wanted the word "metal" to be in there. Because I was into axes and hockey, I thought of the word "blade" and put them together to get Metal Blade. I didn't think of it at the time in terms of being a real record label; I just wanted to call it something fun.

From my perspective, I was still just trying to help out the local scene. I didn't think I'd ever own a record label; I was still way more into the journalistic aspect of what I was involved with. I'd started doing a little work writing for *Kerrang!* That's where I thought things were going to go.

But I couldn't ignore the fact that when I put out the compilation record—which was called *Metal Massacre*—it sold out on the very first day. At that time, I thought 2,500 records was a hell of a lot of copies, and in the context of the day, when independent records might shift five hundred or a thousand copies, I suppose it was. Just getting to that stage was pretty overwhelming for a young guy like me.

I remember sitting in Oz Records, in June of 1982, a week or so after I received delivery of the record, staring at this gigantic pallet that was stacked with vinyl and ready to get shipped out to the distributors. Even then, it was hard to believe I'd actually done it. *Well, Brian, you made a record. That's kind of crazy.*

Important, Greenworld, and another importer/distributor called Jem took the lion's share of the 2,500 copies, a small portion of which were exported to Europe. I can't recall what the exact splits were, but I remember that I kept perhaps a hundred of them for mail order, promo, and to sell in the store. On some levels, the birth of that record was organized; on others, it was very much a seat-of-the pants experiment.

A few weeks after the release, I started getting phone calls from the distributors. "Hey, we need some more of these. Can you get them?"

"Well, no! I have no money! Until you pay me for what you already have, I can't do anything."

I was experiencing first-hand one of the unfortunate laws that fledgling operations face. Back then, everything was on a ninety-day billing cycle. That meant I would have to wait until *they* got paid before *I* got paid. That presented a significant problem, since

people wanted copies of a record that I had no way of delivering.
I was stuck. Demonstrating a degree of business naiveté that was
consistent with many aspects of that first release, I eventually
started avoiding those people's phone calls.

It took a little while, but eventually, Jem, which was a little bigger
than the other two distributors, came to me and said, "Why don't
we license this from you, and then we'll do all the manufacturing
on our own?" They obviously saw the potential, and I wasn't aware
enough to recognize what I might be losing by giving them that
kind of control. Being as all-out-of-options as I was, I said OK. It
seemed like the only way to actually get more records made.

※

In the top floor office above the Oz Records store was a young
lawyer who was just starting out. Being a big music fan, he would
often come in and hang out in the store during his lunch breaks.
Eventually, a few weeks after I'd put the first record out, he asked
me, "Do you have, like, contracts for any of this stuff?"

"No," I said sheepishly. "Are you kidding me? I can't afford to
hire a lawyer!"

"Look," he said, "I'm starting out; you're starting out. If you
want contracts drawn up for this stuff, I'll charge you ten dollars
per hour to do legal work."

Making an instant mental note of my emptier-than-empty bank
account, I still thought, "I *think* I can afford that." And, with that,
we did a handshake deal. That guy's name was William Berrol.
He's still a lawyer today, representing several huge music acts, and
he's *still* Metal Blade's attorney.

William Berrol

*I had just started practicing law at that time and had decided to go out on
my own rather than working for a firm. So I rented a little office in Topanga
Canyon in this little wood building. The rent was three or four hundred
dollars a month, which was less than what I pay for my cell phone bill
now! There were two appeals. One was that there was a record store there.*

I thought, "Well, I don't have any clients, so I might as well be somewhere where I can go check out records." The other was that another friend of mine had an office in the same building, and he was a very well-known radio programmer in LA in the late seventies and early eighties.

Brian was working behind the counter at Oz Records downstairs, and he looked very much as he does now: black t-shirt, and just...Brian. We talked every other day; it was kismet for both of us. At one point he said, "I kind of have this decision to make..." He was referring to the possibility of putting out another edition of the Metal Massacre *compilation, with basically no money to do it. From what I understood at the time, he wanted to expose as many bands as possible, with the ultimate aim being advancement of the genre. And that made sense even to me, as a fan of only the more commercial bands at the hard rock end of the spectrum.*

Anyway, he didn't really even know he needed to have contracts with these bands until I said, "I'd like to think there might be a degree of future success, so you can't just put out music without some kind of agreement with these people." He said, "Well, I don't have any." And I said, "Well, I don't have any clients." So, it was a great combination right from the start.

※

Now that there was legal counsel in place, I had to start going back to all the bands to tell them we needed to create contracts. As I recall, everybody was cool with the idea except Steeler. Similar to Mötley Crüe, they had started to take off a little around that time and, as a result, they hedged their bets, backpedaled, and let me know they didn't want their song on the compilation anymore.

Of course, I had no choice but to be fine with that. I wasn't going to force them, and their getting signed was only a good thing for the movement. For the second pressing of *Metal Massacre*, I brought Black 'n Blue, who were friends of mine, to replace Steeler.

Meanwhile, Jem—the company to which I'd handed over the licensing in the absence of any other means of getting the record out there—seemed very enthusiastic. In addition to handling all the distribution, they seemed like they wanted to make a big priority of the release and to do lots of promotion.

When they got hold of it, they changed the album cover. I think they felt the original was too cheap looking. With Black 'n Blue on there, in addition to an updated version of "Hit the Lights" by Metallica, everything was feeling very positive.

When the record came out, I think it did pretty well. I say "think" because, to this day, I have no idea how many units of that second pressing were manufactured. Believe it or not, I was never paid or accounted to! In truth, I didn't really care about whether I personally made anything; I was still just trying to promote the scene. I was less impressed, however, that the bands hadn't made anything, and that I didn't have the means to do anything about it. That's just one of the many lessons I learned in the early stages of putting records out. As I remember, Jem eventually went out of business, and we were able to get the rights back to press the record a third time, but that was a little further down the line.

Chapter 3
BUILDING THE BEAST

One of the many great aspects of working at the record store was that, as I was importing all these records, I also picked up a copy of each one for myself. I started assembling an insane collection pretty quickly. I had everything that came out during the whole NWOBHM movement. Because I'd become friends with the guys at Shades records in London via my tape trading exploits, I was also collecting all the 45s that were coming out over there around that time.

I was just dying to get over to Europe. It was killing me that I couldn't be there and be part of the amazing scene I was so invested in. Still fueled by jealousy after getting that call from Lars a year or so earlier, I called John Kornarens one day and said, "We're going to Europe!"

In October of 1982, having scraped together enough money to get super cheap plane tickets, John and I embarked on our European odyssey to check out the scene that had inspired us from the beginning.

We had grand plans for when we got there, and a major part of our agenda was to visit Shades Records in St. Anne's Court, just off Wardour Street in Soho. We were going to stay with various friends and stick to a strict budget that would facilitate maximum purchases of vinyl to bring back home.

John Kornarens
I remember we hauled over fifty copies of Metal Massacre *in our suitcases. We just ran around the UK distributing it wherever we could,*

including Scotland, where we gave it to some guy in a castle, who then gave us the first copy of the Mercyful Fate demo!

❋

Strangely, when we actually arrived in London, it seemed like the NWOBHM was winding down. It felt like a fast-moving train that we'd just missed. All we found, in a cold and wet London that had very few shows to see, was the empty space that it left in its wake as it pulled out of town.

Nevertheless, we made the best of what there was. That included going up to Newcastle upon Tyne to interview Raven for the fanzine. The conversation took place at the offices of Neat Records, where we were kindly hosted by Dave Wood, the label boss. It turned out to be a hilarious experience. The Raven guys were the nicest people you could possibly imagine, and we were awestruck to even be in a building with such significance to the world of heavy music. But I could not understand a single word any of them said, because they were speaking so fast! I'd recorded the interview and, even when I tried to transcribe it later, it was almost impossible.

I learned something about the UK on that trip that I've kept in mind ever since: the further north you go, the harder it is for Americans to understand people. In fairness, I have also been told by many by British people that the Newcastle accent is often hard for even *them* to understand!

Two thirds of the way through the trip we went back down south, where I spent literally every last penny I had on vinyl at Shades Records' warehouse on the outskirts of London. I was twenty-one, it was my first time in Europe, and the chance to buy great vinyl had completely overridden common sense when it came to working out how much money I was going to need for the rest of the trip. This was long before credit cards or wire transfers, so there was no point in calling home to talk to my mom about getting more money. I just thought I'd somehow figure it out.

John did exactly the same. For the last few days in London, we were almost completely broke. We had just enough to stay at a very modest bed and breakfast—one room, two beds, and no TV—but they did at least feed us. We ate as much as we could in the morning, and then had just enough left to buy a loaf of bread and some cheese to eat during the day.

A few interesting things happened during those last few days in London. John, being a huge UFO and Scorpions fan, had somehow managed to get in contact with Uli John Roth. Don't ask me how he did it, but the next thing I knew, Uli, nice guy that he was, invited us down to his house, where he was living with Jimi Hendrix's ex-girlfriend.

John and I borrowed enough money to get down to the south coast of England, where we were ushered into a beautiful house and fed lunch. Uli told us a bunch of great stories and played some guitar for us, while John and I sat there wide-eyed, thinking, "Wait until Lars hears about *this*!" It was surreal. It made no sense that he'd bring in these two dumb kids out of nowhere, any more than it made sense that Lars would have been hanging out with Diamond Head. It was all a reflection of the spirit of warmth that permeated the whole scene.

When we returned to London, John and I had nothing to do until our flight home. We had bags of vinyl, but no record player to hear any of the music. Among all the LPs was a lone cassette tape that turned out to be the first demo by the band Mercyful Fate. Since John had brought a cheap tape recorder, we were able to sit in our room at the bed and breakfast and play this demo tape over and over. "Oh my god," we thought. "This is the heaviest thing *ever*!"

※

The reason we'd managed to get such a good deal on plane tickets in the first place was that we'd gone through Toronto. On the way back home, having ditched most of my clothes at the bed and breakfast so I could fit all the vinyl in my suitcase, I got pulled aside by customs. Any band, or anyone who travels through Canada, will tell you that, as nice as Canadian people are, their border guards are tough. The customs guy started going through my bag. Although I'd unwrapped it all in an attempt to make it look as if I hadn't just bought these fifty singles and thitry albums, it still must have been pretty obvious.

At the time you could only bring in, I believe, 300 dollars' worth of goods without incurring some kind of fine. I had clearly spent a lot more than 300 dollars, but I certainly didn't have any money left to pay any fines. "So you bought all these over there?" the customs agent asked me. "Oh no," I said casually. "People gave us most of it for free." But he wouldn't let it go.

"How much is all this stuff worth?"

"Two hundred dollars, maybe?"

"I don't know. It looks like a lot more than that to me."

I said nothing and tried to stay calm, but on the inside, I'd never been more nervous in my life. The very idea of losing these records, after having gone all the way over to London and sacrificing basic necessities like food to get them, would have been unthinkable. After what seemed like an eternity, he nodded. "All right, you can go." John and I walked away with our vinyl, but I was prepared to go to jail to keep those records!

Once I was home, I couldn't deny that the whole trip to London left a bittersweet taste in my mouth. It was great to have been there and to do what we'd done, but that sensation of feeling like things were winding down was hard to dismiss. People's attitudes were definitely changing; heavy metal wasn't getting blanket approval over there anymore.

A particular encounter we'd had in London stuck in my mind. John and I had briefly met Geoff Barton, who worked at *Sounds* and later *Kerrang!* As I mentioned, it was he who was rumored to have coined the phrase "The New Wave of British Heavy Metal" in the first place. We'd been excited to meet him, but he seemed less than thrilled to see us. We wanted stories, but he didn't have any. Instead he said something like, "You know, I didn't ever really like any of this stuff. I was just doing it to create sales and some buzz. I'm more into KISS and the seventies stuff."

John and I were shocked. The English press is what it is. They've always liked to build things up and then tear them down. At that precise moment, in late 1982, they were just at that point where they'd started tearing the scene down. I was particularly crushed when I read the review of *Metal Massacre* in *Sounds*. They trashed the whole thing and gave it a one-star rating. That was devastating because I was a huge fan of *Sounds* and had helped them with features in the past. I couldn't help but wonder whether the review spoke more about the magazine's view of the overall scene than the actual music on the record.

❋

Despite the disappointments, once I returned home, I was even more energized to boost the scene in LA. "If it's dying down over there," I thought, "maybe what's happening here could really become something."

I received an interesting call from Greenworld distributors not long after I got back, and I now see that it definitely pushed me a lot further down the road to creating a full-time record label. "Look, we know you don't have any money," they said, "but you seem like you know what you're doing when it comes to these bands. We'll give you a pressing and distribution deal if you'll bring us more stuff." That was like flipping a switch in my brain. "All I need to do is find the bands, and you'll spend the money to manufacture, distribute, and promote? I can do that!"

I started going to groups like Bitch, who were friends of mine. "If you guys can make some recordings," I'd tell them, "I've now got a way of putting them out." I was just beginning to make a *conscious* move toward developing something more sophisticated by encouraging bands to go beyond single-song contributions and put together EPs, or even full-length albums. The only factor that dictated which option would happen was how much money was available for that band to record.

Bitch was the first. The band members scrambled enough cash together to go into the studio to record the *Damnation Alley* EP, which was released at the very end of 1982. Soon after, Demon Flight did the same, recording the *Flight of the Demon* EP before we started thinking about putting together *Metal Massacre II*. Both EPs did pretty well. I don't remember the exact numbers, but I suspect that a couple thousand of each was made, which was huge for bands of that kind back then.

An Interview with Betsy Weiss of Bitch

Give us a sense of the scene in LA in 1980. What, if anything, was going on?

Pretty much the beginning of the metal scene in LA was just starting in 1980. The NWOBHM was just beginning to infiltrate its way into the US, and I think those bands were a major inspiration for Bitch guitarist and founding member David Carruth. The seventies glam, new wave, and punk bands were pretty much on their way out, and the eighties were primed for the birth of the LA metal scene.

How did the band come to be formed?

David Carruth and drummer Bobby Settles knew each other from Texas, where they both resided. They were both very active in the music scene there. They each moved out to LA independently, and eventually caught up with each other. David was in a band called Badaxe with Slaughter bassist Dana Strum. He left that band with the intention of forming his own hard rock/metal band. David and Robby originally wanted it to be an all-male band called Bitch, but when they answered my lead vocalist ad, all of that changed. I was fresh out of a ska band called The Boxboys, which started out as a rock/new wave group, but decided to change to ska music because, according to them, there were already too many rock/new wave bands with female singers in LA. I tried it. Ska was definitely not my style, so I went looking for something else and hooked up with David and Robby after they answered my ad in Music Connection advertising myself as a "charismatic lead vocalist looking for a hard rock band."

Was music always what you wanted to do?

I came from a family where my father was a professional jazz musician and my mother a stage actress, so entertainment was something I was always exposed to. I could always carry a tune and had good projection. I was in my high school glee club and joined some garage bands after that. Then I took some basic vocal lessons so I could "find my voice." The Boxboys and then Bitch were really my first performing bands.

How did the connection with Brian and Metal Blade come about?

David and Brian were friends before the inception of Metal Blade Records. David knew Brian from the record store Brian ran, Oz Records. They specialized in imports, picture discs, European and rare releases—all of which David was an avid collector of. When Brian started up Metal Blade—running it out of his mother's garage at first, by the way—he knew David was forming a metal band and asked him if we wanted to be on the first Metal Massacre compilation. When the band had finally written enough material for an album, Bitch became Metal Blade's first full band LP vinyl release.

How difficult has it been being a woman in the metal business? Has that changed over the years?

When the metalheads first got wind of a black-leather-and-studs band with a female vocalist, I don't think people thought I could pull it off. But once I hit the stage, their minds changed. I wasn't really taken seriously at first, but the fact that I could back up the image with talent and stage presence was really in my favor. When the band first started out, people thought I was an actual dominatrix. They had no idea I was the lead singer for a metal band. Once things started to progress, I felt like I was accepted into the "heavy metal club." I felt like one of the guys. This has changed a lot over the years, in terms of the acceptance of women in the genre. People are a lot more open to it, whereas before, they were skeptical that a woman could really pull it off.

> **The band had some management issues back in the eighties. Would you say that hindered your progress?**
> *We did hook up with a management company that gave us some bad advice and sort of put us on hold for a period of time while they re-tooled our image and music. People were starting to wonder what happened to us. They were nice people; they just had the wrong vision for us. When we finally parted ways with them, the band got back on track again.*

What I was slowly starting to find out via the process of releasing records was that there were other people scattered around the country who were into the same thing. I was starting to see that record stores like Oz were popping up in Texas, Chicago, and all kinds of other places. There was suddenly a growing scene beyond LA. All kinds of fanzines started to appear, like Ron Quintana's famous *Metal Mania*, which launched in San Francisco in early 1982.

That year was a significant turning point. It was the first time I started thinking of what I was doing as something that could potentially extend beyond my immediate surroundings. I suppose that realization may have made the idea of running a full-time business seem potentially viable.

I had a conversation with my mom about the idea of taking some time off from college so I could focus all my energies on the various enterprises I had going. I was hesitant to broach the subject, but, to my surprise, she was absolutely fine with it. She could see that I was passionate about what I was doing. She was also aware that working in the record store, producing the fanzine, and now developing a label left little time for me to continue with my studies. Something had to give, and that something was college. It was a season of change, in many ways. I took a big leap, but I found myself flying solo, as John opted to step away.

John Kornarens

Eventually I kind of lost interest, mainly because I didn't really like Brian's musical taste at the time. I didn't think he was as deep as me! Cirith Ungol

and Demon Flight, man? I thought I was more discerning. Plus, I had my
college degree, no contract with Metal Blade, and a different direction to
go in.

In addition to the shows I promoted around LA to support the
Metal Massacre records and enhance the profiles of bands like Bitch
and Metallica, I had the idea to put on a *Metal Massacre* show at a
club in San Francisco called The Stone. The lineup was originally
supposed to be Bitch and Cirith Ungol, but then Cirith Ungol
dropped off for some reason. I asked Metallica if they wanted to do
it and, of course, they agreed. By this stage in their development,
the band consisted of James, Lars, Dave Mustaine, and Ron
McGovney. They had not yet recruited Cliff Burton into the lineup.

None of us had any money, so the whole exercise was a
somewhat risky proposition. While Metallica had been playing
around LA in the latter part of 1982, they had definitely been the
black sheep of the scene there. Ratt was starting to make serious
waves and Mötley Crüe was blowing up, so the scene in town was
gradually moving that direction, and away from the heavier stuff.
But Metallica was *so* heavy. Their set in those early days consisted
of a Blitzkreig cover, a bunch of Diamond Head covers, and a
small handful of originals, like "Hit the Lights." They just did not
fit in. Most of the promoters thought they were a punk band.

I knew there was an early scene brewing in San Francisco.
Exodus was up there, and a few other bands were starting out.
All of it was boosted by Ron Quintana's first fanzine, which had
promoted, among other things, Metallica's *No Life 'til Leather* demo
from the summer of 1982.

We piled into a bunch of cars and went up to San Francisco.
The first band (which shall remain nameless) played, and was
just awful—so awful that I remember noticing that most of the
audience turned their backs.

Then Metallica came out, and it was complete pandemonium.
There wasn't a huge number of people there—maybe 200—but
these kids just went completely nuts the moment they started

playing. It was eye-opening to me, and very different from the reaction they'd been getting in LA. I thought, "Something is definitely happening here."

It turned out to be a huge watershed for Metallica, and, by extension, heavy music in general. For the first time, I started allowing myself to think that they might become a serious band. That felt incredibly gratifying, because I'd been involved from the start. On the other hand, I realized that, as much as I wanted to continue working with them, and vice versa, there was a big problem: neither of us had any money to make any music. At one point they came to me and said they'd worked out a deal with some studio in LA to record an album for ten grand. "That's awesome," I said, "but who has a *thousand* dollars, much less ten grand?" Obviously, that never happened. I couldn't offer them any security, but I knew their music *had* to be recorded.

During this period of late 1982, I'd been gathering music together with the idea of releasing *Metal Massacre II*. One of the submissions I received was a three-song demo from a San Francisco band called Trauma. It was recorded pretty professionally, and their management told me they were coming down to play a show at the Troubadour. He suggested I come out to see them.

I went to the show and the band was OK, but certainly not amazing. The bass player, though, was fuckin' out of this world. You could see there was something completely crazy happening on his side of the stage. He was wearing a blue denim vest and wide bell-bottoms, and really stood out. I discovered his name was Cliff Burton.

Cliff impressed me so much I agreed to put the Trauma song "Such a Shame" on *Metal Massacre II*. Shortly before it was released, I was hanging out with Lars Ulrich one day when he said, "We need a new bass player."

As they'd started to practice more and hone their respective abilities as musicians, the Metallica guys realized that the only member who wasn't developing was bassist Ron McGovney. Ron was a great guy, super cool and totally into it, but Lars told me they felt that, for the newer material they were writing, Ron just wasn't up to it from a technical perspective. Lars asked me if I knew of anyone else who would be a good fit. "Now that you mention it," I responded, "there's this band called Trauma from San Francisco, and their bass player is phenomenal. They're coming down again for another show, so you guys should go check them out."

I saw Lars and James at Trauma's next LA show. Maybe five minutes into the set, Lars turned to me and, with a smile, said, "That's going to be our new bass player."

An Interview with James Hetfield of Metallica

What was Metallica prior to the offer to contribute to *Metal Massacre*?

Lars and I had met in LA, jammed with each other, and discovered that it wasn't really a fit yet. We weren't very good at what we were doing. I had started a different thing called Leather Charm, played some songs with people, tried to be a singer, and was really just desperate to get into a band. But then Lars called me and said, "Hey, I'm still looking to put a band together and I have a blank space reserved on a compilation record that my friend Brian Slagel is putting out. I just need a band. Are you interested?" I said, "Of course!" That's when we got back together. It wasn't like he had joined my band or I had joined his band. It was just these two guys who were interested in that kind of music. Lars definitely turned me on to a variety of metal bands from England that I'd never heard of and, while "Hit the Lights" was a song that originated in Leather Charm, Lars and I revamped it a little bit and made it heavier—in line with the music we were enjoying at the time.

How much do you recall of the process of recording "Hit the Lights?" Presumably it was quite primitive?

It was done on a Fostex 4-track! We'd laid down the main instruments: Lars with his drums, then I did the guitar and filled in on the bass. Then I did another guitar track and sang, obviously. We bounced some tracks down and it didn't sound amazing, but we had one track left for a solo. We didn't know who was going to put the part on there until Lars said, "Hey, I've got a friend who can rip a solo." Literally on the way to the studio to deliver the tape to Brian, we went over to Lloyd Grant's house, and he just plugged in all his pedals and went crazy. Then we walked to the studio and handed Brian the tape while Betsy from Bitch was in there recording vocals for the song they were doing for the compilation. It was very primitive, and Brian, who was frustrated with the format, probably at some point said, "This is not useable; it's not going to sound great." But he managed to get it on there and got it sounding decent enough so that we could basically start our career.

And then you re-recorded it for the third pressing of
Metal Massacre?
Yes; we had a little more quality at that point and included Dave and Ron on it.

Prior to that first show in San Francisco, how was the LA audience responding to you?
Well, we definitely felt—we experienced a sense of alienation. We would show up at clubs, and we certainly didn't look the part. We didn't have the glam look, and I remember getting thrown out of the Troubadour once because, at sound-check, they thought we were a punk rock band. They said, "Hey, we only want rock here, so get out." People didn't know what to do with us, and we weren't embraced at all. But when we went up to the Bay Area and experienced that scene, it blew our minds. When Cirith Ungol couldn't make it to that first Metal Blade–sponsored show, we just hopped in Ron McGovney's pickup truck with the camper on the back and a trailer for our gear. I absolutely remember loading into that gig. Our first time there was very memorable.

Was the difference in the response that significant?
Absolutely. We saw kids showing up in denim vests. They didn't care too much what they looked like. They were there to hear and experience the music. They weren't there to hang out at the bar to see who was there, or who they could pick up. There was no posturing. Back in the day, "Kill the posers!" was the chant of the heavy metal community. Everyone was there for the music, not to be seen.

Later, in 1982, Brian was instrumental in the idea of Cliff Burton joining the band. How, exactly, did that happen?
We were searching for a bass player and, yes, Brian suggested we go and see Trauma. Just like he had done by bringing LA bands to the Bay Area, it was the same thing in reverse. A bunch of Bay Area bands were coming down to play for the LA scene. So Lars and I went to the Whisky to see some bands, one of which was Trauma, and I remember

we thought, "OK, well the songs are so-so." It didn't blow our minds whatsoever, but as we were chatting away and having a drink, all of a sudden we heard this noise. We thought, "Oh, this dude's doing a guitar solo." It sounded really interesting; it sounded weird. It sounded like a different kind of guitar. When we looked, it was the bass player with this big red mop bouncing up and down with these huge elephant bells on and a wah pedal, doing this insane solo. We just looked at each other and said, "We've got to get this insane maniac in our band. He'll fit right in."

Cliff was the complete package of sound and look, then?

Yeah. He didn't fit in with anything we'd seen before. He didn't even fit in with his own band! They had a certain look and he was just…Cliff. Sonically, he was aggressive; he was head-banging the whole time with his giant hair. It was a whole package, yes. And after meeting him and talking with him, he was an extremely down-to-earth guy. Somehow Brian must have known he was going to fit in.

The end of 1982—when you moved as a band to San Francisco—would seem to be the point at which you parted ways with Metal Blade. At any point, was there a conversation about Metal Blade being your record label going forward? Was that on the table at any time?

That's a great question, because I was completely divorced from the business part of the band. Lars was the one who knew more about it. He had followed Diamond Head and Motörhead around and learned not just how to play, but also how to manage a band and how to get a band out there by doing gigs. The business side was kind of his forte from the beginning, so I don't know why it wasn't talked about or what happened with that, but once we met with Cliff and he said, "I'll join your band if you move up here," it was an extremely easy decision. So I don't know why we weren't connecting with Metal Blade at that time; it's a good question.

How much involvement have you had with Brian since?

Brian's the guy he's always been. I'm sure he's seen me change quite a bit, from this shy kid to the front man in Metallica. But he has remained the same, and I have the utmost respect for him in that he has done so much for this kind of music. Through the ups and downs of the record business, and the ups and downs of the popularity of this kind of music, Brian has continued to fight and do what he feels is right. He's a survivor. Yes, he's a big music fan, and he loves discovering stuff and putting it out there. But, besides putting newly discovered bands on the map, he has taken bands who were forgotten and then gone and bought rights and pressed CDs of bands that we would have never otherwise heard on CD. A band like Riot is a great example. I love that he has put out music by bands like that on a format that we can all enjoy.

Could you sum up Brian's significance, in terms of you being where you are now?

There's no doubt about it. We might have still been trying, or at least still been looking for that opportunity, but he was the one who, for some reason, believed in us—and particularly Lars—at that time. Lars was a true metalhead. He knew his metal, and he loved it and lived by it. Brian was the same way. I'm sure Lars was hounding Brian the whole time at the store saying, "Hey, have you heard this? Hey, what have you got? Hey, what's next?" So Brian knew and trusted Lars because he'd been trying so hard. How can you deny that kind of hunger and drive to put a band together? That Brian would save a spot on a record for a band that wasn't even formed yet was a huge leap of faith. So I'm extremely grateful for him giving us that opportunity. It's an honor to be part of that first Metal Massacre, no doubt about it!

A welcome byproduct of my time with Metallica, and exposure to the Bay Area scene during those years, was my involvement with Exodus. I became good friends with those guys during 1983 and 1984, and we talked seriously about signing them and doing a record.

Meanwhile, a friend of mine in New York—Todd Gordon, whom I'd gotten to know as a pen pal—wanted to follow in my footsteps in terms of starting a small label.

Todd had always been very kind to me. The first time I ever went to New York I called him up, asking if he knew anywhere I could stay. He said, "Yeah, you can stay with me!" I crashed with him at his parents' house in Westchester, and we became good friends. Todd had a friend who was, in some way, connected with the San Francisco scene, and who also had a little money.

As Todd and I talked about Exodus, he said, "I'd really like to start this label, and I have a little financial backing. Would you mind if I signed Exodus instead of you signing them?" Todd was such a good dude, and had been so good to me, so I said, "Sure, man. Go ahead." I probably should have discussed us doing it together, but he had the connection who was willing to front the money. If it came down to it, I probably could have found a way to finance it, but it was Todd who ended up signing Exodus and releasing *Bonded by Blood* in 1984 on his own Torrid label. If I knew then what I know now, I might have done things differently, but sometimes it's good karma to just let things go. In any case, I love the Exodus guys, and they were going to get more money with Todd than they would have gotten from us at that time.

Chapter 4
CARVING OUT A NICHE

As 1982 turned into 1983, things started to get very busy. It was still just me in a little room behind my mom's house. I had no air conditioning, which was no fun, given that Woodland Hills gets up to 100 degrees in the summer. I was doing everything myself: the artwork, the typesetting, approving all the information, checking the mastering, checking the recording—I was a one-man record label, and I was learning most of it as I went along.

But I didn't care. I'd get up in the morning, work until two o' clock in the morning, go to sleep, and then repeat. It was constant—seven days a week—but it was fun because there were just so many new bands appearing.

I'd officially quit school in 1982. In early 1983, I also quit working at Oz Records, simply because I literally didn't have enough hours in the day. The fanzine fell away due to time constraints, but it was also becoming expensive to produce. I had called in favors early on to get the issues out there, but, as it got a little bigger, people were understandably reluctant to keep doing the work for no money. By mid-1983, all the extracurricular activities had dropped away, and I was working on the label full time.

※

Just around the time I was becoming increasingly consumed with the label, I was flipping through *BAM* magazine and noticed an article about a band called Armored Saint that had just won a battle-of-the-bands competition. They looked super metal. There was a phone number in the ad, so I called them up: "Hi, I'm Brian Slagel," I said. "I've just put a couple of these *Metal Massacre* releases out. You guys look great, and I'd love to come see you."

"Oh, sorry," they told me. "We've got to take six months off because our bass player just messed up his hand, so we can't play any shows for a while."

Joey Vera, the bass player, had been playing in a group with Tommy Lee. They had done some sort of gig in the mountains near Mammoth, and had driven up in Tommy's tiny hatchback. After the gig, Tommy picked up some girl and wanted to give her a ride back, so Joey agreed to sit in the back of the car. Tommy lost control on some ice when they were heading home, flipping the car, and sending Joey flying through the glass hatch back, which shredded the tendons in his hand.

Eventually, after a few months had elapsed, I got a call from Armored Saint's manager saying they were back, the bass player was healthy, and they were playing a show at the Troubadour the following week. I went to the gig and was blown away.

Joey Vera (Armored Saint)

One night, in late 1982, we played a show at the Troubadour in Hollywood. It was probably the band's tenth gig ever. During our set, we saw this dude standing back at the bar. He was wearing an Iron Maiden shirt with the sleeves cut off. He was wearing these leather-and-spike gauntlets on both of his forearms. He waited until we came out of the dressing room after our show and introduced himself. He was intimidating to see at first; he's taller than we are! Plus, those gauntlets! But he was just down-to-earth and very cool. Brian Slagel offered us the opening track on Metal Massacre II *right there on the spot.*

I was obviously into the whole European style of metal, and, as good as Metallica was at that time, the band's sound was evolving, and James was still developing as a singer. But Armored Saint had it *all* together. John Bush was an amazing front man with a phenomenal voice, the music was really heavy, and they looked great on stage with two guitar players. It was the first time I'd ever seen a band in a club that already looked like an arena band. "Holy shit," I thought. "These guys are *amazing!*"

As it turned out, they were from Pasadena and had initially only played shows around that area. Then, when they won the battle-of-the-bands competition and got the ad in *BAM*, things really started happening. Recognizing the huge potential, I immediately said, "OK, we could do songs for *Metal Massacre*, and maybe we could do even more after that—perhaps an EP."

John Bush (Armored Saint)

The first Saint show that Brian came to was at the Troubadour around Christmas of '82. We knew who he was and were very excited by his presence. He seemed equally stoked and suggested we work together. The story was apparently that Mercyful Fate was supposed to lead off Metal Massacre II, *however, the band and management had a falling out, and Brian only had contact with the management people, who were uncooperative. It ended up being the right place at the right time for Saint.* Metal Massacre II *was our first official exposure, record wise, to the wider world. It was our first step as a baby band.*

One of the things that differentiated Armored Saint from many of the bands around at that time was that they actually had a little bit of money. That really helped, because money was the single biggest problem, closely followed by getting access to studios where we could record. I was trying to get loans all the time, but nobody was ever going to give me any real money because I had no assets. Even my mom, being a single mother who worked hard to keep the household together, didn't really have anything to give me.

At that time, it was really expensive to record. You couldn't just book a studio and make a record for one or two thousand bucks. Fortunately, an engineer and producer—a guy named Bill Metoyer—appeared just when I needed him. He had a band called Dietrich that he'd worked with and that he had helped record an EP. The band itself wasn't anything special, but I couldn't help noticing that the sonic quality was really strong. When I talked to

Bill, it became apparent that he could facilitate some affordable recording time. "I work at this place called Track Record," he told me, "and the owner there is cool. We can go in overnight and record stuff really cheap." When I say "cheap," it was going to cost maybe 200 bucks a night, which, at that time, was at least affordable. The alternative was six or seven hundred bucks per day.

Bill Metoyer

The summer after I graduated high school was the best time of my life, full of concerts and fun. I was not ready to go back to school. I was having too much fun. But I had a partial scholarship to USC, so I went to please my parents. I lasted two semesters and dropped out. I promised my parents I would go back after a year, but, in the meantime, my classmate and buddy who originally got me the job at Music Plus (Jim Faraci, who, by the way, produced a few bands for Metal Blade, including Lizzy Borden and Trouble), was attending engineering school at the time. He seemed like he was having a blast learning the trade, and it was a way to stay in the music business. I found a school in Hollywood called the University of Sound Arts, enrolled, and that was the beginning of my career in engineering and production.

My electronics teacher at the University of Sound Arts, Tom Murphy, was also the co-owner of Track Record. I'm not sure how long the studio had been around before I met Tom. I know it started as an eight-track studio, and by the time I met him, it was sixteen-tracks. When Tom and his co-owner, Bob Safir, needed interns at the studio, he would recruit one of his students. Tom asked me to be an intern. Initially I was getting coffee, cleaning the toilets, and setting up microphones. There was no pay, but I would get to use the studio when it was available.

Track Record was a nice recording facility with a good Neve board and switch-tape. Bill knew how to work everything, and he was also a metal fan. It all came together perfectly. The release of the Armored Saint EP in 1983, produced by Bill, was another significant turning point in the trajectory of Metal Blade. It was a great band that had a lot of buzz. This was the first time— having put out five or six records—that I felt somewhat legitimate.

"Maybe," I thought to myself, "I've actually built a real record label!"

Metal Blade seemed to have a real synergy going on in that era. In addition to Armored Saint and Metallica, there were bands like Savage Grace, Omen, Bitch, and Steeler, who all hung out together pretty much every weekend. The epicenter of the scene seemed to be Bitch frontwoman Betsy Weiss's mom's house in North Hollywood. It was just a fifteen-minute ride from venues like The Whisky and The Troubadour. Literally every weekend, there would be some Metallica members or some Armored Saint members there; we all hung out and formed a true community.

There were a million parties there, and one of them was legendary. We were all there partying until four or five in the morning. A big thing back then was a dogpile. Someone is thrown on the ground, and everyone else just jumps on top of them. It was raging that night, and I had kind of passed out on the couch for a while, only to wake up to Motörhead's "Ace of Spades" accompanying a massive dogpile of thirty people. At the end of the song, when we got to the bottom of the pile, it turned out that Phil from Armored Saint was lying there with a badly messed up leg. The party was over, and everyone left. Armored Saint had a show the next day, and Phil ended up sitting on a chair playing the guitar.

Lizzy Borden

All the local bands that were affiliated with Metal Blade at the time: us, Armored Saint, Bitch, and Metallica, would show up at Brian's house for horror nights. We'd all sit around watching these really terrible horror movies like Dr. Butcher. It was so fun, and the camaraderie at the time was really important. None of the bands sounded the same, and I always thought that was really interesting. But all of us hanging out in the same place, watching the same movies, having a few beers—that was probably the equivalent of UK bands going to the pub.

An Interview with Joey Vera of Armored Saint and Fates Warning

What was your musical background, and where did heavy music first start to fit into your world?

I began listening to hard rock around 1976: Queen, Thin Lizzy, Aerosmith, Sabbath, Ted Nugent, and KISS. Once I started playing bass in 1979, I got more into heavier bands like Priest, UFO, Rush, Van Halen, and AC/DC. There was a circle of friends, and we all listened to and shared the same music.

Brian describes the beginnings of a scene in the early 1980s in LA; what are your recollections of what was happening there at that time?

The hard rock scene in LA in the late seventies got a shot in the arm with the rise of Van Halen. After that, you saw more bands coming up with a heavier sound. We'd go see Snow, Quiet Riot, George Lynch's Xciter, and Smile, just to name a few. Then, by 1980, we all discovered the NWOBHM and Kerrang! *magazine. Slowly, most of the young bands coming up were basically trying to recreate what we saw in* Kerrang! *and in the UK in general. It was all totally new and exciting. There was a great buzz in the air when you went to go see bands play in the clubs. By 1983, there was a full-on scene where everyone who was into seeing high-energy music could now describe it as heavy metal. Before that, you would not use that term to describe what you were into. Being right in the scene and being in a band at that time was pretty wild. It really felt as if it belonged to only us. Little did we know how huge heavy metal would really become in the years that followed. But at that time, it just felt right.*

You've had various crossovers with Metallica over the years. How did they come about, and at what point were you closest to being in the band?

We became friends with them just before they moved up to San Francisco. We had the most in common with them, since the Hollywood scene was becoming somewhat of a spectacle. After they moved up north, we stayed friends and did several gigs with them in the Bay Area. Then in 1984 and

'85, we toured with Metallica and W.A.S.P. That tour was legendary, and we and the Metalli-boys, of course, hung out most of the time. We'd take turns camping out on each other's buses for late-night travelling parties. It wasn't uncommon for me to wake up on their front lounge seats in a different city the next morning, and vice versa.

Years later, after the accident involving Cliff, the band had been auditioning bass players. It was very hard on them, jamming with mostly complete strangers. They wanted to play with some of their friends. So Lars called me one night, explained this to me, and asked me to come up and "see what happens." At that moment, I was halfway through the making of our third record for Chrysalis, Raising Fear. After sleeping on it and much soul-searching, I came to the conclusion that I was not ready for that change in my life. I wasn't ready to bail out on my childhood friends and what we'd been working on for the past five years. My gut said that making the decision would only be out of opportunity and not out of what my heart knew, which is to make music that I love and that I am a big part of. I had to call Lars back and politely decline his offer. He understood completely. I will always be humbled by that offer.

Describe the role Brian and Metal Blade played in making *Symbol of Salvation*, the landmark record that emerged from a set of tragic circumstances.

The band had been dropped from Chrysalis in 1988 right after the Raising Fear *cycle. Frankly, at that time, we were glad about it. We were very unhappy with the label. Little did we know how hard it would be getting a new deal in the late eighties when hair metal was the soup du jour. But we wanted to get on another major label.*

We were in writing sessions and playing label showcase gigs from 1988 until 1989 when, in late '89, our guitarist, Dave Prichard, was told he had leukemia. After losing his battle in a bone marrow transplant, Dave passed away in early 1990. At that time, neither Jeff Duncan nor Phil Sandoval was in the band, so we decided to put the band off indefinitely. After a few months, Brian Slagel came to us. "You have to make this record," he told us. "You have too many great songs that you wrote with Prichard." Brian convinced us to get it together.

Metal Blade paid for a guitar-auditioning period where we were flying players in from all over the place. We played with some really great guys, but there was always a subtle element that didn't feel right, so we decided to bring back the two guys who had already played with Dave before: Jeff Duncan (1988) and Phil Sandoval (1982–1984). Then, suddenly, it felt like home again. Brian hooked us up with producer Dave Jerdan (Alice in Chains, Jane's Addiction) and we made Symbol of Salvation for Metal Blade in 1991. Brian was very, very close to the making of this record. From the song choices to the recording and mixing, to the artwork—very involved. So much so that we butted heads quite a bit about decisions! But in hindsight, I realized it was only out of the complete passion he has for our band.

Has being in several bands on the Metal Blade label ever made your relationship with the label more complex?

Complex is a good way to put it! But it's never impacted anything negatively. I appear on many different Metal Blade releases and have worked closely with many of their staff members, who are just some of the best people you'll ever meet. They are all true music fans. I even met my wife, Tracy, at the label. You can imagine doing business with your wife. I am the artist and she is the label. Complex? Yes, but I have had a great relationship with everyone who's come and gone there, and I've seen the label go through ups and downs. I can honestly say they have one of the best staffs I have ever seen anywhere.

Your music and the bands you play in cover quite a variety of styles (all of them under the broad umbrella of heavy music). Is this variety something you need?

Yes, I think it is. I didn't realize this, though, until I was forced to try new things once Armored Saint broke up in 1992. Since then, I thrive on doing different things and challenging myself. I think I would get bored if I was to end up only doing one thing over and over. It keeps the music interesting, as well as my playing.

By 1983, it seemed like I'd become something of a go-to guy for emerging bands. People were starting to see what was going on with the scene in LA, and demos started arriving in the mail for review. There was such a variety, and it was getting really exciting to see what was going to show up next.

At some point toward the middle of that year, I went out to watch Bitch play a show at Radio City in Anaheim. I hadn't been out to Orange County too often, but I'd heard that Bitch had played several shows there in the past. They were headlining on that particular night. I got there early, and there were a bunch of other bands on the bill—none of whom I'd ever heard of. But I always stayed and paid attention to who was playing. It was an open-minded approach I felt I *had* to have if I wanted to discover the best bands around.

My patience paid off when it turned out that one of the bands playing was Slayer. As soon as they went on and I saw these four guys with crazy makeup and tons of smoke on stage, I thought, "Holy shit!" Until that night, I was completely unaware of them; I had no clue. They were absolutely unique.

Similar to Metallica, Slayer's set consisted of a bunch of cover versions, and maybe three or four originals. Kerry King and I still argue about it to this day, but I swear they played "Phantom of the Opera" by Iron Maiden. He swears they didn't. Either way, whoever's right, I know they played an amazing Iron Maiden cover, which was enough to tell me this band was *incredible*.

Kerry King (Slayer)

For us, no scene existed in LA. It was where all the so-called hair bands and glam bands were getting big and, to me, the biggest crossover act at the time was W.A.S.P. They were heavy and had a different imagery, but they still had makeup and teased hair. But we were always more of an Orange County band. We owned the Woodstock. Once we got some popularity, we played there every couple of weekends.

Jeff and I were very aware of the Metal Massacre series, and we always thought we were as good as, if not better than, most of those bands that

were on there. We perceived it as an opportunity. Labels weren't paying any
attention, so we were all very excited about Brian's interest. Brian and I hit
it off; we've been friends ever since. It's always fun to find people to share
your common hobby. Metal was his hobby, and we happened to play metal.

I went to see the Slayer guys backstage after the show, and I
spoke to their then-manager, who was an eighteen-year-old kid
named Steve Craig. "I thought the band was amazing," I told him.
"I do these *Metal Massacre* compilation albums, and I'd love to have
Slayer on one. What do you think?" He agreed, and we exchanged
business cards.

A few weeks later, I went to see them again, and then I went
a couple more times after that. A few more originals started
appearing in their set each time, and it became obvious that this
band had really serious songwriting potential. Not all young bands
possessed natural ability like that. "If there's any way you guys
could record a whole record," I promised, "we would put it out."
They were really serious about the idea.

Again, there was no other way for a band like Slayer to get heard
outside of LA, so they worked with Bill Metoyer on a track called
"Aggressive Perfector," which would ultimately end up on *Metal
Massacre III.* They had a really good experience working with Bill, so a
few weeks later, Tom Araya's dad gave them three thousand dollars to
go into the studio. That was a hell of a lot of money in those days, but
it didn't buy a whole lot of studio time—maybe two weeks in total.

Bill Metoyer

*The first time I worked with Slayer is when they came in the studio to
record "Aggressive Perfector" for* Metal Massacre III. *While setting
up, they would play Judas Priest songs, lick for lick, perfectly. They were
just a bunch of kids then. If fact, they showed up with squirt guns and
were running around the studio, squirting each other with water. The only
problem is, they would run in the control room, squirting water near the
thousands of dollars' worth of electronic equipment! I almost had a heart
attack. The other fond memories were of their contests to see whose farts
smelled the worst.*

Kerry King (Slayer)

As I remember it, when we recorded "Aggressive Perfector" for Metal Massacre, *Brian offered us an album deal on the spot. But he didn't have a shit-ton of funding; he was just starting out as well. He contributed something to* Show No Mercy. *I know my parents contributed, and I know Tom himself, or him and his parents, did, too. Between all that, we got it taken care of.*

The strangest part about the whole recording process for Slayer's debut album, which would be called *Show No Mercy*, was that all the cymbals had to be overdubbed. Everyone played live, but since Dave had such a huge drum kit, and the studio was so small, the sound of the cymbals was bleeding over into all the other microphones—to the point that the sound would have been unintelligible if it had been left as it was.

Bill came up with the idea of idea of overdubbing them, which meant that Dave had to play the entire record without any cymbals—which is insanely awkward. And, even more awkward, was playing them in isolation later. I still have a picture of Dave in my head, standing there waiting for the time to come to hit each one. It was the weirdest-looking thing, but apparently the only solution.

I was not a qualified producer at all, but because I was wearing every hat humanly possible, another of those hats that I ended up wearing was "producer." It was a role I took on out of sheer necessity, since *someone* needed to do it. I can't play an instrument, but I did know what sounded good. That's how I ended up producing the first Slayer record.

Kerry King (Slayer)

I don't recall specifically what input Brian had into the production. I do know that we've always been so hard-headed—especially me and Jeff—but, that being said, I'm always open to an idea. I think you're foolish if someone's got an idea and you don't listen to it. But unless it was a slam-dunk of awesomeness, we'd usually just ditch it.

The guys in Slayer were just eighteen-year-old kids, but they were so incredibly smart and creative, even then. They were doing stuff that was far beyond what anyone was doing at the time. Every day I went in and watched them put material together, and I was always blown away by how professional it was.

When the record was finished, I went into the office at Greenworld, our distribution company. This was the first time I was comfortable saying, "I think we *really* have something here." When the record came out, and a buzz started, my feeling was confirmed. While there was a lot of excitement surrounding Slayer, it wasn't easy to get *Show No Mercy* into stores because of the lyrical content of most of the songs. Mainstream audiences weren't into it, but the underground was freaking out.

As far as sales were concerned, if you sold ten thousand copies of a record on an independent label back in 1983, you'd be dancing on the tables. After a few months, *Show No Mercy* had sold in the region of three thousand, which was, far and away, the biggest thing we'd done. By the end of the first year, we'd sold five thousand.

Things really started to take off when we began licensing material to companies overseas. Roadrunner and Music for Nations were the main two, both of which went on to become huge companies. The Slayer record was the gateway, because it gave us a degree of legitimacy we didn't previously have. In addition, because I was sitting on so much good material, I was able to put out two more compilations albums in 1983: *Metal Massacre III* at the beginning of the year, followed by *Metal Massacre IV* several months later. It was all coming fast and furious.

※

If you look at the releases on Metal Blade in 1982 and 1983, the vast majority of the bands were based in the LA area. That, I suppose, was reflective of how the eighties metal scene evolved.

Gradually, though, I started getting demo tapes in my mailbox from bands far away from LA. The excitement and anticipation I felt was just like it was in my tape-trading days as a teenager, only now these bands were wanting the attention of the record label I'd somehow created. I'd go out to that same mailbox at my mom's house, and there would be demos from bands like Overkill from New York and Obsession from Connecticut—even Aloha, Marty Friedman's first band from Hawaii. I listened to *everything*.

Some of the demos we received were really very good. One of the first that really grabbed my attention was from a Chicago band called Trouble. As I remember, the demo hadn't been sent to me directly by the band; it had come from a friend of mine in Chicago who knew about them. It consisted of two live shows, and maybe two or three songs they'd recorded in the studio.

I listened, thought it sounded great, and then called the band. "Your stuff sounds amazing," I told them. "I'd love to do something with you guys." It was always the same conversation at the beginning: money. But, at that point, we'd sold just enough records that there was at least some income coming in, so we had a very small budget for selective recordings. As we talked, it became apparent that, whatever happened, they weren't going to be able to record in Chicago. Studios there were too expensive, and it was virtually impossible to get any time out there. I suggested they come to LA to record, so they piled into a van, drove to California, and we did the first Trouble record in a week at Track Record. They were the first band from outside of LA that we'd signed, recorded a full record for, and released it. We got an amazing reaction to that record.

Everything went into high gear from 1984 onward, because there were just so many great new bands. We signed more acts and sold a few more records, which, in turn, increased the funds we had available to invest in recording. It was a snowball effect.

Chapter 5
GROWING PAINS AND PLEASURES

During my last days working at Oz Records, I'd noticed these kids who used to come in from time to time. They'd buy some stuff, but didn't really talk until, finally, one guy who turned out to be a drummer came in and said, "You know, we're in a band. We have a demo tape, but we're a little scared for you to listen to it!"

"Why?" I asked. "Let me hear it!"

With them begging me not to, I put it on in the record store while there were probably thirty other people browsing. It was Lizzy Borden's "Rod of Iron."

Lizzy Borden

I got into a few different bands trying to figure out what to do, and then my drummer friend, Joey Scott, and I joined another band and started playing the Hollywood circuit. And that's when everything became more focused. We could see there was a scene there that hadn't quite happened, but it was starting to boil. It was still very small, and everyone played with everyone else. We started at the Troubadour, but at that time it was set up like a folk venue. It certainly wasn't set up like it later would be. We were on the same bill with heavier bands like Slayer and others who'd later be called speed metal. It was all just one basket then; there was no separation.

We were rehearsing in a place called Harlequin in the San Fernando Valley, and it was there that someone told me about this guy who put out records by local bands. At that time, the idea of putting out vinyl seemed impossible. But when someone told me about Brian, I thought, "OK, where is he?" I was told that he worked out of a record store. Joey and I went down there to Oz Records, just walked in with our demo and said, "I heard there's a guy who works here who puts out local bands."

The guy at the counter said, "Yeah, that's me." So I handed him the demo and started looking through the imports when all of a sudden our music started playing over the house system. It was the Rod of Iron demo, which had four songs. He played them all, right then and there. Then he came over and said, "One of these songs will be on the next album. Just go record it again and bring it back."

Thus began a long relationship with Lizzy Borden. After we put out "Rod of Iron" on *Metal Massacre IV,* which came out at the very end of 1983, we followed it up by releasing the debut EP, *Give 'Em the Axe,* which Metal Blade issued in 1984.

Lizzy Borden

Our first EP, Give 'Em the Axe, was funded entirely by Metal Blade and was postponed, initially, because Brian had no money. Meanwhile, we had already finished three albums! The EP was the first time we took recording seriously. We had so little experience. Initially, we found a sound working with Bill Metoyer at Track Record, but we couldn't get it right. Then Brian came in and said that the recording was there, but the mix wasn't. So he brought in Ron Fair, who ended up mixing it.

⚉

Sometime during 1984 I remember getting a copy of *Kerrang!* magazine and seeing a review for a band called Hellhammer. The reviewer basically said it was the worst record that had ever been released, so I immediately thought, "I have to hear this!"

I listened to the record and thought it was amazing, so I contacted their label, Noise Records. "Let me license this for the US," I pleaded. They liked the idea and we came up with a reciprocal arrangement where they would agree to license a couple of the *Metal Massacre* compilations in Germany. It was the beginning of a great relationship, and Noise had some amazing bands on their roster. In addition to Hellhammer, we'd eventually work with Celtic Frost, too. We also started licensing some things from Roadrunner in 1984—the first of which was Silver Mountain, Yngwie Malmsteen's first band. And, again, *they* were licensing some material from us.

Another one of the demos that landed in my mailbox in 1984 was an amazing set of five or six songs from a Connecticut band called Fates Warning. It was freaking amazing. Fortunately, they had recorded their demo with a reasonably high standard and it was my feeling that, if they went in and recorded maybe two more songs, we could mix an album and put it out with little need for alterations. It was one of those rare occasions where you receive a demo that's so good you can actually make a record out of it. Bill Metoyer and I mixed the material in Los Angeles ahead of the release of Fates Warnings' debut full length, *Night on Bröcken*, in September, 1984.

Bill Metoyer

I remember when Brian handed me the demo and told me he thought the band was awesome and that he liked every song on the tape. He said he wanted to release it as an album, but thought the sound could be better, so he asked me to re-mix it. When I heard "Damnation," I fell in love with the band.

Jim Matheos (Fates Warning)

We had no idea what we were doing. Recording that demo was the first time any of us had been in a "real" studio, and our inexperience, to me, is fairly obvious.

We were just five very young music fans with a wide range of influences. We decided very early on that we wanted to write original music rather than play covers mixed with a few originals in hopes of getting "noticed" at some point. We would often go see another local band, Obsession, and when they landed a spot on Metal Massacre II, *we thought they'd hit the big time. It showed us you could break out of the local scene.*

Getting on the next Metal Massacre *became our main focus. We finally made it onto* IV *after sending that original demo to Brian. I remember after we sent it, I received a contract in the mail a few weeks later. No phone call, no cover or introduction letter, just a contract. Of course we were excited, but there were also lots of questions. So, one evening I called the number on the contract, thinking I'd have to speak to a lawyer or secretary, or maybe just get an answering machine. Brian answered, and we ended up talking a long time, not only about my questions concerning the contract, but about music, bands, and the then-current metal scene. So that was pretty cool, and I don't think that happens a lot these days!*

Shortly after Fates Warning and Trouble entered the picture, I received another demo from a Canadian band from Montreal called Voivod. They were a tricky one because they didn't speak any English. Nevertheless, we managed to put an agreement together. Because of the language barrier, I was never sure if they were totally clear about what was going on. Despite the problems, we did the *War and Pain* record with them, which turned out great. Unfortunately, that was the only album we ever did with them because they had a manager come in who started scrutinizing our contract while, in the background, they apparently had other labels interested.

�֍

Another notable relationship from 1984 came with my involvement with a band called Metal Church. I had known Kurt Vanderhoof for a long time, dating back to early conversations we had around the time of *Metal Massacre*. We had discussed the idea of including an instrumental track from Metal Church, which, at the time, didn't even have a singer. They were going to be on the record, but then Kurt got cold feet. He saw too many uncertainties. They were up in Seattle, and they had interest from a few other labels, so they pulled out at the last minute.

In 1984, things came full circle, and we managed to negotiate an arrangement to record "The Brave," which would end up appearing on *Metal Massacre V* in May of 1984. In retrospect, when you look at the artists that appeared on *Metal Massacre V*, there's no doubt that it was one of the more significant editions of the compilation series. Voivod, Omen, Metal Church, Hellhammer, Overkill, Fates Warning—all bands that would go on to achieve considerable significance in later years.

In the meantime, Slayer was getting bigger and bigger after *Show No Mercy.* They'd been on tour in early 1984, using Tom Araya's Camaro with a U-Haul trailer to carry the gear behind. That was the way it had to be done for evolving bands in that era. There were no, or very few, booking agents operating at that time, so a lot of the early tours were organized by a band's manager—or, in Slayer's case, by their excellent road manager, Doug Goodman.

Touring, in general, wasn't such a huge part of a band's existence then, in comparison to what it is now. While there were scattered scenes in places like Chicago, the East Coast, and the West Coast, the idea of trying to do a national tour was relatively unheard of for small metal bands in the eighties. Instead, bands might make regional trips—LA to Texas, for example— but anything beyond that didn't make much sense, given how little money was at stake at the time. There was just too much uncertainty in terms of how many people might show up. One night there could be a few hundred people; other nights there might be twenty. In fact, I've seen Slayer, on several occasions, play in front of twenty people or less! Fortunately, Doug Goodman was really good at calling clubs and making sure the guys in the band got paid what they were supposed to.

After the album came out, Slayer had written a couple of new songs. "We're not ready to do another full record yet," they explained, "but what about maybe going in and recording them?" We had a little money, so we were able to pay for enough time to record "Chemical Warfare," "Captor of Sin," and "Haunting the Chapel," all of which sounded so great that we figured we might as well put them out.

It seemed like a good opportunity to keep the great momentum going that Slayer had created. Back then you, could put physical product out there much more quickly. It was one form—vinyl—

and there wasn't as long a lag time as there is now for pre-promotion and everything that comes along with releasing material in the current environment. Back then, you'd just finish something up, get the artwork done, get it pressed, and then release it—all within a month or so. Now it's at least a three-month process from the point at which an album is recorded until it appears on the market. Slayer's *Haunting the Chapel* EP was recorded quickly and released right away. It kept the band's profile high, and it maintained the flow of money back to my label.

I say "my" because, despite the fact that Metal Blade put out a lot of albums and was involved in all manner of two-way licensing deals with Europe, it was still just me. Granted, Bill Metoyer was deeply involved, since almost all the recording and engineering was done at Track Record. But in terms of the day-to-day running of most of the label's activities, it all came down to me, and that included my fair share of producing at least some aspects of the majority of these records.

Bill Metoyer

I don't like to say that I was the in-house producer. It's just that, since I worked at the company, I was OK with doing jobs fairly cheaply, because I liked the bands and wanted the work. Even when Metal Blade started paying for the recordings, the budgets were small. We would do a lot of recording in off hours when the studio time was least expensive. There were many nights of mixing that started at midnight, and then I had to wake the bands up to listen to their mixes because they were asleep on the control room floor!

Chris Barnes (Six Feet Under and formerly of Cannibal Corpse)

As a teenager in Buffalo, looking in magazines—which I didn't have many of to guide me to good music—I always found myself drawn to Metal Blade records that had the names Slagel and Metoyer on them. That started when I went to a record store and chanced upon some Metal Blade stuff one time. It was the best stuff I picked that day. That became my guide for how I wanted to find stuff. The first record I picked up was Witchkiller's Day of the Saxons.

While there was more money to invest in doing more projects on an increasingly larger scale, I was still operating out of the little room at my mom's house. I was working eighteen and sometimes twenty hours per day, seven days a week. Fortunately, I was the kind of guy who could be organized when it came to what I saw as important. At that point, with a fast-growing record label, I had to know what was going on. If you'd walked into my bedroom around that time, however, you probably wouldn't have considered me "organized." There were clothes everywhere because I didn't consider putting them away important, and didn't have time for it!

I had to do all the other stuff that the business demanded, and that included figuring out who was going into the studio when, dealing with manufacturers, getting test pressings, and checking them. I was also doing all the promotion, so I'd be calling radio stations, putting albums in mailers, and shipping stuff out constantly.

Then, in the evening, because there was always somebody recording something, I'd make the thirty-five-minute drive from Woodland Hills down to the studio in Hollywood. I'd be there from seven until maybe two in the morning, offering whatever input I could during the production process. I'd go home, grab a few hours of sleep, get up, and do it all again. That was my life for the entire year. It was crazy busy, but also crazy exciting.

As the overall scene was becoming something significant, there were several sub-scenes boiling up. Thrash was just one of them. Slayer was causing a buzz, while Metallica and Anthrax were putting out their records and getting a lot of traction. Then you had the LA metal scene where Mötley Crüe and Ratt were leading the way. On a wider scale, bands like Judas Priest and Iron Maiden were putting out huge albums and playing arenas. *Everything* was getting bigger, and the focus now was on a much broader geographical area than just a couple of US cities and Europe.

As such, 1984 was an incredibly historic time to be involved in heavy metal music. Everyone inside the scene just lived and breathed it. It was a lifestyle as much as it was a taste in music. The standard uniform of jeans, band t-shirt, and tennis shoes meant that metal fans, much as they are today, were instantly recognizable.

It really felt like "us against everybody else," which only galvanized the movement. Metal felt like an exclusive club, so there can actually be some pitfalls that come with success. I remember a quote by Dee Snider from Twisted Sister, which I read after they'd started to get big and finally got a good review in a major magazine. "That's what killed our career," he quipped in reference to the positive press. In retrospect, he was right. As soon as anything that was previously seen as rebellious gets accepted in any way, it ceases to be rebellious.

※

Everything in terms of how I did business back then was shortsighted. I wasn't ever looking at the broader picture of where things could potentially go, and I still had no idea that what I was working on was going to be a job for life. Consequently, some of the early licensing deals and contracts were not done with a long-term future in mind, and that was really just naiveté on my part. I didn't always capitalize on some of the contracts and licensing deals I set up. That meant that, later, I lost the rights to certain recordings because the paperwork allowed them to revert to the artist after a certain period of time. That was just one of the many mistakes I made along the way, purely because I didn't know better. It certainly wasn't the only one.

Sometimes records don't get done on time, and a release date is missed as a result. That happened now and again but, in those days, I never saw that as a complete disaster. Today it *definitely* would be. Back then I just thought, "Ah well, it'll come out next week rather than this week. It'll still shift a few thousand copies."

Dealing with money was one of the steepest learning curves in those early years. There were definitely times when I owed a lot of money for studio time or typesetting, and, because records were sold on a consignment basis, it was sometimes hard to know exactly where we stood financially. From month to month it was hard to plan things when I didn't know if I was going to get paid for, say, the 3,000 copies of a particular record that we'd shipped, or for only 1,000 because the remainder had been returned. At times I came up very short.

As a result, sometime toward the end of 1984, I remember calling Greenworld and saying, "Is there any way you can give me a flat amount every month? Then at the end of the year we can take a look at everything and hopefully we're not too far away with the numbers?"

Because I had no way of getting a credit card or a bank loan to fall back on in the lean spells, I wanted to avoid situations where one month I'd get paid 15,000 dollars, and the following month only 5,000. I remember going into banks to try to get a loan and explaining the way the business worked. They didn't want to hear any of it. And who could blame them? I had no collateral—*no anything.* The car I was driving was a Plymouth Duster that my mother had bought me for a few hundred dollars. It ran, but it wasn't worth anything. Eventually, Greenworld agreed. That moment was significant, because managing money, or having no money at certain times, was the single biggest issue in the business.

Despite the financial issues, in October of 1984, I bought a ticket to fly over to London again. This time, I was by myself. The purpose of my trip was twofold: First, I was meeting with Martin Hooker at Music for Nations, the label that was licensing some of our music in the UK. Secondly, I was getting together with all the business people I knew over there, like the folks at *Kerrang!* magazine. There was actually also a third motivating factor for the trip: Dio was playing a couple of nights at the Hammersmith Odeon, and then, later that week, Iron Maiden was playing the same venue.

I arrived in London on a Sunday with no hotel reservation and no credit card. It was pouring rain, and it quickly became apparent that there were no hotels available. None *anywhere*. I was asking people on the street what was going on. Finally, somebody said, "Oh, there might be a hostel up the street that has a room," so I walked half an hour, in pouring rain, with a gigantic bag, and finally got to this place where they said, "Yeah, we have one room." It was this tiny room at the top of four flights of stairs, but it was fine for what I needed.

Even though the whole NWOBHM had pretty much died down by 1984, the wider metal scene was really starting to erupt. It was an amazing time to be in London. There were metal stores everywhere. Every corner kiosk had tons of heavy metal t-shirts, and the fashion of studs and leather jackets ruled the day.

I had arrived amid a new golden era of heavy metal, and seeing it all really motivated me. I'd been doing Metal Blade on my own for a couple of years by then and, as much as I enjoyed it, it wasn't as if it was easy. I still didn't know where I was going, and I was still stuck in my mom's garage. But those ten days in London, seeing Dio and Iron Maiden twice, were ten of the greatest days of my life. I returned to the United States with a renewed determination to do everything I could for the metal scene and to make the business work financially. Sometimes you just need a bit of motivation to be reminded of the potential of what you're doing.

Thankfully, only once or twice in the next few months would I sail close to the wind from a financial perspective. The important thing was that, with a degree of security, I'd be able to continue pressing records and finding new bands from either a demo or one of the many live shows I was going to whenever I could. It was probably a fifty-fifty split in terms of how I discovered bands I wanted to have a conversation with about being on the label. Bands that weren't from LA—as was the case with Fates Warning or Trouble—would be heard via a tape. But the local bands, like Omen or Savage Grace—I'd decide what to do with them after seeing a live gig. There's still absolutely no formula, even to this day. If I like a band, I want to work with them. I never looked for anything specific. If I put something into the tape player in 1984 or look on the internet today, if I listen to it and like it, I'll go from there. There was never a master plan, and there still isn't.

Today I can tell very quickly if a band I hear is something I'm going to want to work with—usually within fifteen seconds. But, back in 1984, it was a little bit different because I'd pay more attention by spending half an hour listening at a show or listening to at least a couple of songs from a demo tape. Inevitably—as was the case with Mötley Crüe and Metallica—there are bands that slip through your fingers for one reason or another. But those were few and far between in the very early days. At the time, there was really no competition other than from Megaforce Records on the East Coast.

The only band that I didn't get that I wished I had was Megadeth. It was between us and a brand new label called Combat, which was part of the Important distribution firm that we'd started out working with. Late in 1984 they'd decided that the whole metal thing was starting to happen, and they wanted to get in on it by creating their own label. The first band that came onto their radar (and ours at the same time) was Megadeth. In the end, it came down to just a thousand dollars. We had offered them seven thousand dollars, but Combat offered eight, so they went with Combat.

With hindsight, especially given what Megadeth became, I've often thought, "Well, maybe I could have gotten a little more money together." But really, at that time, seven thousand dollars was absolutely the most money we had ever offered anybody. Most of the stuff we were doing involved spending $1,500 to maybe $3,500, at the high end, to make a full record. Seven grand was a lot of money. I remember Dave Mustaine writing me a really long, heartfelt letter saying how he really wanted to be on Metal Blade, but it just wasn't meant to be.

Megadeth's debut, *Killing Is My Business...And Business Is Good*, was released in June, 1985, and the rest is history. The same applied to Metal Church, Overkill, and Anthrax, all of whom I talked to. In all three cases, it was just so much easier for each of them to go with labels that were close to their respective home cities. As bummed out as I was to not be able to work with these bands, their reasons made total sense. In those pre-internet days, when even long-distance calls were prohibitively expensive, the country seemed like a much bigger place. Instead of focusing on what I didn't have, I moved on and continued pushing what I did have. And Slayer, even at that time, was an entity that I knew could be the biggest band on the label.

By early 1985, *Show No Mercy* had sold close to 30,000 copies, which, for an extreme band on a small label, was a very significant number. Slayer had everything together. They were unbelievably talented musicians, and what they were doing live was so good. They were incredible. They weren't these charismatic guys running around on stage, and Tom wasn't the best front man by any means. But the amount of energy those guys created when they got on stage together was something I'd never experienced before. Magic happened every night.

The Slayer guys, especially Jeff Hanneman, were really into the punk scene. There was an underground movement happening and, somehow, Slayer had become friendly with the guys from D.R.I. and had asked them if they wanted to do a show together. "I'm not sure how that's going to go," I remember thinking, but it was amazing, and they were all super nice guys.

I decided I wanted to work with them but, back in the eighties, a punk band just couldn't be affiliated with a label that had the word "metal" in it; it just wouldn't work with the respective fan bases. These scenes were far too disparate, and the respective ideologies had no crossover—at least, that was how it was seen at the time. D.R.I. said, "We'd love to sign with you, but we don't want to be on Metal Blade."

"I get that," I told them. "What if we sign you, but have a different label name?" They went for it. Remembering my experience coming up with the original name for the label, I did a bit of due diligence and launched some research to make sure the name I had in mind didn't already exist. It didn't. I figured out the basic registration paperwork, filed a simple D.B.A. (doing business as), and came up with what was essentially a sub-label called Death Records. It was specifically created to sign and release the music of punk-orientated bands that I didn't want to let go just because they weren't making strictly metal music.

Around the same time, I caught wind of what Corrosion of Conformity was doing over in North Carolina. Somebody turned me onto their first record, *Eye for Eye*, and it didn't seem like there was much going on; it was released on a tiny independent label. I loved them and immediately reached out, but they, too, were deliberating. "We don't really want to sign with a metal label," they told me.

"Well, we just signed this punk band called D.R.I.," I explained.

Fortunately, the two bands knew each other, and that was enough.

Corrosion of Conformity signed to Death Records, too, and we slowly but surely started to sign a few more crazy bands that were great, but wouldn't have fit comfortably on the main Metal Blade roster. It's funny because we only ever signed maybe a dozen artists to Death Records, but three or four of them are in *Decibel* magazine's Hall of Fame! We were doing *something* right.

The good part about creating a sub-label of that kind was that nothing changed in terms of my day-to-day workload. The contracts were the same, and I was still the person dealing with the details. Everything was exactly as it was with Metal Blade releases except, when it came to the physical record, there was a Death Records logo instead of a Metal Blade logo.

※

Slayer was due to go into the studio in May of 1985 to record the follow-up to the *Haunting the Chapel* EP.

At the beginning of that year, Armored Saint—for whom we'd done the self-titled EP and the debut full length, *March of the*

Saint—signed to Chrysalis Records. The A&R representative there was a guy named Ron Fair. Ron was a really great guy who loved metal, and he was helping us out wherever he could. In addition, he was a seasoned record producer who knew his way around the studio.

John Bush (Armored Saint)
At that time, everyone's goal was to make an independent record that would hopefully lead to a major record contract. It was the way. Brian knew that also, and wished us well.

I was talking to Ron one day, and we started discussing Slayer. He, like most people, thought *Show No Mercy* was great, and I asked him if he'd consider coming in and providing some real production input, while the band, Bill Metoyer, and I did what we do. "Absolutely," he said, and he was there for the entire process as an engineer and co-producer. That was a game-changing moment. As good as the first two Slayer releases sounded, despite budgetary limitations and a few technical conundrums we'd run into along the way, we wanted whatever they did next to sound even better. Ron's presence really helped us. Even his interpersonal skills seemed to bring more out of a band that was already far ahead of most of its peers in terms of discipline and work ethic. It may be that, because of his experience and cache in the business, the Slayer guys listened to him more than they did me and Bill. Whatever worked best was fine by me!

Plus, Slayer came into the studio as a more seasoned band. They'd kept getting better live, and their technical skills had improved as a result. In the time that had passed since *Show No Mercy*, they had really honed their sound. Instead of grabbing at a variety of different influences, they now knew what they wanted; they had an identity, and it was our job to capture that live sound on the record that would become *Hell Awaits*.

Kerry King, who was always the driving force in the studio, had developed an ability to stand back and look at a record through a wider lens. In addition to taking care of lyrics, songwriting,

and playing his instrumental parts, Kerry was also very aware
of sequencing, flow, and production gimmicks. In fact, during
the process of making that record, we respectfully ripped off so
many production tricks from Judas Priest: use of reverb, balance,
and fade—all kinds of subtle nods. And that was all Kerry, who
was a huge Judas Priest fan. Tom didn't write lyrics and wasn't
particularly involved in the songwriting process (although some
of his ideas and connections were used for the album's cover
art). Even some of the bass parts were difficult for him to grasp. I
remember Kerry ended up playing a few small bass parts along the
way.

Jeff Hanneman was a vital component in the overall makeup
of Slayer. He was the riffmeister; he just came up with all these
amazing guitar parts and had a unique punk background that
complimented Kerry's metal leanings. In some ways there were
parallels with Metallica, where James was more of a punk guy
and Lars was the metal guy. As was the case in both bands, when
you fused those two influences together, something amazing was
created.

Then there was Dave Lombardo, who, while he didn't write
songs, was incredible at embellishing what was already there with
unbelievable drum fills that only he could possibly invent and
execute. Slayer has always had a really interesting dynamic.

When I listen to *Hell Awaits* now, I'm really proud of it. As
controversial as this may sound, it's still my favorite Slayer record.
Reign in Blood is obviously the greatest speed metal record of
all time, but it's all one pace. *Hell Awaits* had slow stuff and fast
tracks, and I liked that contrast. Interestingly, a couple of songs
that would later appear on *Reign in Blood* were conceived during
the *Hell Awaits* sessions. In fact, we had every intention of putting
"Altar of Sacrifice" on *Hell Awaits* but, if memory serves, the
vocals weren't quite together, and we ran out of time to get it
right.

Bill Metoyer

I think Slayer progressed with every record I worked on with them. I consider Hell Awaits *the best album they did for Metal Blade, and, judging by how many musicians—including Phil Anselmo and drummer Gene Hoglan— cite* Hell Awaits *as an influence, it was hugely important. But hell, all the records were evil! The first words you hear on* Haunting the Chapel *are, "The holy cross, symbol of lies, intimidates the lives of Christian born." Since I was raised Catholic, those are some of the most evil words you could say! The thing that gets me is how many people out there still think* Reign in Blood *was the first Slayer album.*

When *Hell Awaits* came out in September of 1985, I was acutely aware that it was a very significant moment in the trajectory of this little record label that was rapidly expanding beneath my feet. I'm no producer, per se, but having spent enough time in studios, mixing and mastering, you can get so close to the material for so long that you're pretty sick of hearing it by the time it's released.

When *Hell Awaits* came out, it was different. I couldn't stop listening to it. In fact, it was pretty much all I listened to for three or four weeks. It was so good, which I say both as someone who'd been involved with the process *and* someone who's purely a metal fan. It was certainly the best thing Metal Blade had ever been involved with. Back then, I considered it one of the best albums I'd ever heard.

Interestingly, from a sales and distribution perspective, there were a few issues with getting *Hell Awaits* in stores, due to the cover art and the lyrics. That wasn't new with Slayer; we'd had some problems with *Show No Mercy*, but everything was still very underground at that time, so it wasn't as if that record was going to get into mainstream stores either way.

Hell Awaits was obviously less underground, and I recall some resistance with getting the album into retail internationally. But, overall, it was such an important record that, even if they didn't bring it into the stores initially, they eventually did because people wanted it so badly. You could say that simple demand forced the record *out* of the underground.

The end of Metal Blade's involvement with Slayer after *Hell Awaits* was a bit of a strange time for me. They had been talking to a few people and, because we were all young guys and didn't really understand the business inside out, I was helping them and trying to guide them. It was no secret that Rick Rubin really wanted Slayer. But there were other labels that wanted them, too.

And then fate intervened. At some point toward the end of 1985, I had to go to Europe for a music convention. Rick Rubin met with the band while I wasn't around. I wouldn't go so far as to say that was intentional, but it was definitely…interesting. In my absence, Rick convinced the band to sign with him, which they obviously did. Credit to Rick Rubin: he was going to get the band however he could, but that triggered a weird situation between me and the guys that lasted for maybe a year until the various rights and future rights were resolved to everyone's satisfaction. Everything turned out fine in the end.

Kerry King (Slayer)

Brian knew most of the songs we had for Reign in Blood because I know that we recorded them, albeit primitively. The funny thing is, when Rick Rubin got in the picture, he contacted Dave first. To this day, I don't know how that happened, because Dave was never the most outgoing of the four of us! But he made the connection, and we got hooked up with Rick. They had major distribution, and that was attractive to us, so we went down that route.

I should say that I had no qualms with Slayer signing to a major label because I knew—*everybody* knew—it was going to happen sometime. The reality is that sometimes you just can't keep a band. It generally comes down to economics. A major label has the ability to offer a group the kind of money that young men can't refuse, and it's great for those bands to get that opportunity. I was just a small label with a few acts. I couldn't compete with the majors, and made no attempt to do so. We eventually lost more than 20 bands to major labels at one point or another in the following years. Some did well, Slayer being one of them, and others didn't do so well. You win some; you lose some.

In the overall context of Metal Blade, obviously Slayer was a really big commodity, but, at the same time, we had so many other bands that were making records. As huge as Slayer was, we still had Omen, Corrosion of Conformity, Fates Warning, Lizzy Borden, Nasty Savage, Voivod, and Trouble, to name just a few. When I look back on it, the roster was growing exponentially at that point.

Chapter 6
"I" BECOMES "WE"

It was right around that time, in 1985, that Metal Blade went from "I" to "we." While Bill Metoyer was essentially a quasi-employee by virtue of how much he was doing in the studio and helping out with other things, it was still largely a one-man show. That was the year I made the move out of my mom's garage and into a one-room office in Reseda, where I brought in a part-time assistant.

Our new location was right across the street from the Country Club, where John Kornarens first ran into Lars Ulrich. A scene from the movie *Boogie Nights* was filmed in the donut store that was right next door to our office. It was great to finally have a real base of operations, and the building blocks in place for an actual staff.

Within three or four months of moving into our rented office, we needed even more space. There were a lot of releases coming out, and they were all doing fairly well. As a result, slightly more cash was coming into the business. Metal Blade was finally in a place where we could afford to spend the kind of money on albums that the bands and their music deserved.

By no means, however, was I rolling in cash. While the office was in Reseda, I was still living at my mother's house in Woodland Hills. Everything coming in was going straight back into the business, and I was still in such a state of immersion that I didn't realize I had an actual career. I was still young, about to turn twenty-four, and all I knew was that my life was a lot of fun. I didn't have a lot of time to plan or philosophize too much.

On a wider scale, the heavy metal landscape was changing a little during 1985. The major labels, sensing that metal was not just a quickly passing fad, were definitely beginning to show an interest in signing these bands. Metallica had already been signed to Elektra, and *Ride the Lightning* had come out in the summer of 1984. Armored Saint was out there on a major label, too, so suddenly agents were sniffing around the Metal Blade roster. As time passed, that interest level would steadily increase.

I wasn't dwelling too much on whether major labels were coming to sign my bands. There was no point, because I couldn't stop it even if I wanted to. Instead, I busied myself with finding more great bands and releasing albums that were worthy of Metal Blade Records. One of them was Fates Warning, which recorded one of my all-time favorite albums on the label: *The Spectre Within.*

Another significant moment came with the second Trouble record, which was called *The Skull.* For one reason or another, the recording ran way over time. I can't remember what the issue was—I think maybe they couldn't get the drum sounds right, or perhaps it was some other technical issue. Because they were from Chicago, we only had somewhere for them to stay for a certain length of time. The studio was a dual-purpose facility called Preferred Studios, where they could sleep and record in the same place. It was a slightly shaky arrangement. We'd never used this particular studio before, and we didn't have the easy relationship we'd developed with Track Record over the preceding couple of years.

For whatever reason, I had to leave the recording process to fly to New York before it was finished. When I got back, after being away for four or five days, I opened the office door to find ten people sleeping on the floor of my tiny office. Nobody had told me that the Trouble guys had been kicked out of the studio while I was away. They had simply run out of money and time, and Preferred

Studio wasn't prepared to let them finish with no guarantee of payment. Apparently, Bill Metoyer came up with the idea: "Why don't you just sleep on the floor of the office?"

In the end, the record got finished, and Trouble went back to Chicago. I believe it was the first Metal Blade record that ever went terribly over budget. Even though there wasn't too much money around, we always seemed to find a way.

Trouble is a band that could have and should have been much bigger. We had a similar situation with them that we had with a few other bands on the roster: we'd do a couple of records, and they sounded great, and then someone else (Rick Rubin, in Trouble's case) signed them. Usually they would ultimately get away from their original sound because labels, in the latter part of the eighties, encouraged bands to write radio hits. That was the sad truth of what happened, and it was the downfall of a number of great bands.

Other than maybe some college radio stations, I never gave a thought to whether or not a band of ours got played on the radio. I just wanted to make great records. But I should say that college radio, in those early days, was a vital source of publicity for us. We were forever sending as many things as we could to college stations, since it was one of the only means of elevating some of these bands to any sort of level. To their credit, college radio stations were always willing to play whatever we sent them.

✳

By the latter part of 1986, I felt like the records we were putting out were sounding really good, from a production perspective. It's one thing to put out good music, but for that music to come with the complete package of proper presentation only elevated the status of what we were doing. Omen's *The Curse*, released in October of 1986, is a good example of one of many records that I can listen to now and still think, "That *sounds* incredible."

The same is true of Lizzy Borden's *Menace to Society*, released a month earlier. That was another record that we went to town on, from a production budget perspective, by getting Ron Fair on board to produce once again.

Lizzy Borden

Brian was in the studio with us in the early days because we didn't know what we were doing. He wanted to make sure his money was getting spent well. We played six nights a week and were pretty proficient, but we didn't really have the chops in the studio. We were such a live band, but we really wanted to capture and translate that to a recording situation.

Lizzy Borden was really starting to make some major inroads. They had a great live show and, in keeping with that, were selling out all over the West coast. They were slightly less heavy than many other bands, and they were getting some extra exposure because of it. We even thought they might be the band that would crush all others, but, unfortunately, it didn't work out that way. Lizzy always had the wrong manager or the wrong agents working with him. "It seems like you're shooting yourself in the foot," I used to tell him when he'd bring in some new character who didn't seem to be the right fit.

It's still the case to this day that, with any band, all four wheels have to be moving in the right direction, or else the car is not going to go anywhere. Metal Blade has way more say in these things than we used to. We had people that we liked to work with, and we tried as hard as we could, but, ultimately, it always comes down to decisions that the bands make for themselves. The biggest mistake any band can make is not having someone in the organization with some business sense. It's the business mistakes that will fuck you up, and that's a big reason why so many otherwise great bands fail.

Back in the eighties, none of us were really true business people. It was all trial and error and, in a band environment, you were just really lucky if somebody had the smarts to figure it all out. Sometimes the hardest thing to get bands to understand, even to

this day, is that we—the label, the management, and the agents—
work for them. It's not the other way around.

Just as I've always felt Lizzy Borden could have been bigger,
the same applies to Fates Warning. *Awaken the Guardian* was a huge
record for them and us. They were another band that traveled to
LA to make an album and, in their case, we recorded at Capitol
Records Studios. That was another crazy moment when I had to
pinch myself in disbelief.

We'd been mastering some of our bigger records at Capitol,
under the watchful eye of their mastering engineer, Eddie Schreyer.
Eddie mastered a ton of our stuff, and would later do a lot of
work for Roadrunner, with many gold and platinum records on
his résumé. He was a really amazing guy who we used for years,
even after he'd left Capitol. Through him, we were able to get in to
record at the famed tower. It was a little surreal walking down the
hallway of that legendary studio every morning.

Jim Matheos (Fates Warning)

*I tend to be fairly critical of all my work. It's hard to listen to much of it,
new or old, without thinking I could have done something better or different,
or even, sometimes, not at all. That said,* Awaken the Guardian *is one
of a handful of records I've been involved with that I can listen to and think
there's some things there to be proud of. We're doing a couple special thirty-
year anniversary shows this year where the lineup from that record will be
performing the entire album. It's been fun and challenging to reconnect with
that old material.*

Awaken the Guardian turned out very well, but—a little ironically
maybe—I still go back and listen to the production and feel
like we could have done a little better. But the music itself is
phenomenal—one of the top ten records the label ever put out.
I love seeing albums like that stand the test of time. It's looked
at more fondly now than it was back in 1986! At the time, Fates
Warning didn't really fit in with all the "cool" bands. People
accused them of sounding like Iron Maiden, but, really, they were
much more progressive than Maiden ever was at the time.

Today, many people list Fates Warning as an influence. The album is now in the Decibel Hall of Fame. It's widely considered one of the greatest records of its kind ever made. Fates is another band that could have probably gone to a major label, too, but I really think they and Lizzy enjoyed being on Metal Blade. They were all very good friends of mine; we had a really good relationship and, at the time, everything was going really well for both bands. We were also starting to see that other bands that were signing to major labels weren't quite getting what they wanted or had hoped for. These long-term relationships have been super important to Metal Blade.

One of the things not many people know about Fates is that the original singer, John Arch, has paralyzing stage fright. He can't stand playing live, to the extent that he left the band after *Awaken the Guardian*. You'd never know it if you met him offstage, and you'd never notice it from his performances, either. But he hated it.

✖

By 1986, there were three independent metal labels in the country: Metal Blade, Combat, and Megaforce. All were vying for bands' attentions, and we were all trying to one-up each other while holding our ground in the face of the major labels that were taking an increasing interest in metal acts.

Back when Slayer had been in the studio recording *Show No Mercy*, I'd noticed a kid hanging around the studio. He was quiet and super nice, but was always just there watching. "Look, who *is* this dude?" I asked the guys one day during a break. "Oh, that's our friend Gene," they told me. "He's a drummer. He just wants to watch what's going on in the studio."

The kid turned out to be Gene Hoglan, and I later found out he was in an amazing band called Dark Angel. We ended up putting a song of theirs on *Metal Massacre VI*. When it came time for them to sign a full record deal, having only previously done just the song for the compilation and a demo, all three of the independent labels wanted to sign them. It was a non-contest.

THE NEW
HEAVY METAL
REVUE

$1.00

NUMBER TWO

AUG-SEPT 1981

IRON MAIDEN INTERVIEW!

<u>PLUS</u>! Def Leppard, Motorhead, Girlschool, Angelwitch, Diamond Head, The Rods, Trust, Anvil, Y&T, Raven, & more!

IRON MAIDEN **LIVE IN L.A.**

The second issue of *The New Heavy Metal Revue* fanzine, 1981

Brian interviewing Iron Maiden's Bruce Dickinson in the fanzine days

Where it all began: the first *Metal Massacre* compilation
that launched Metal Blade Records, 1982

Keepsakes from Brian's early days promoting
Southern California metal shows

Brian and Bill Metoyer at Track Record Studio, where most of the early Metal Blade albums were recorded

Metal Blade introduced the world to Slayer and reintroduced classic Alice Cooper albums via deluxe reissue releases.

In the studio: (L-R) Mark Zonder, Bill Metoyer, Brian, John Bush, Rocky George, and Ken Baumgartner

(L-R): Ice-T, Chris Barnes, Brian

Brian presents Jim Matheos and Ray Alder of
Fates Warning with album sales awards

Brian with King Diamond

Brian with Lemmy Kilmister and friends at the
Foundations Forum's F Music Fest, 1996

Brian with Lizzy Borden (L) and Gwar (R)

Brian with L.A. Kings players Luc Robitaille (L) and Steve Duchesne (R)

Brian in the Metal Blade offices, 1990s

Backstage with Metallica (L-R): Lars Ulrich, Brian, James Hetfield, Kirk Hammett (Photo by Ross Halfin)

Brian with Kerry King of Slayer (Photo by Paul A. Hebert)

Brian and his mother, Maren Slagel

The guy at Combat basically flipped out and offered them a ton of money. Back then all I could say was, "Take the money! I can't compete." Although it would have made more sense for an LA band to be on a West Coast label, it worked out fine for Dark Angel at Combat.

Another band from that era was Cryptic Slaughter. I saw them at a few shows, and they had a really good demo. I ended up putting them on *Metal Massacre VII* in 1986. Their sound wasn't conventional. They had a lot of hardcore and punk elements, but there was also a thrash component in there that worked pretty well. I suppose we were more receptive to that because of our forays into the punkier stuff via Death Records. After we signed them to do a couple of albums, they kind of disintegrated.

Back then I would never have suspected that one of their band members, bassist Rob "Blasko" Nicholson, would go on to great things outside the band. In fact, when he was playing bass in Ozzy Osbourne and Rob Zombie's bands, I'd forgotten about his previous life. I met him somewhere and he said, "Remember me? I was in Cryptic Slaughter!" He now manages a bunch of other groups and has done really well.

One of our main sources of finding new acts was from other Metal Blade bands. Bitch, for example, had gone out to play a show in Phoenix. When they came back they said, "Hey, the band that just opened for us was called Flotsam and Jetsam. They're amazing; you should check 'em out."

They had a demo tape at the time called *Metal Shock*, which I listened to and fell in love with. Then I went out to Phoenix to see them live, and they were as amazing as my friends in Bitch said they were. While I was there, I became aware of another band from the Phoenix area, Sacred Reich, that we'd also sign to the Metal Blade roster.

While we'd had a lot of proficient bands on the label by that time, the Flotsam guys seemed even more experienced than some of our existing bands. I immediately talked to them about the idea of making a record, and, because we had some money to offer, we were able to record *Doomsday for the Deceiver*, which was released in July of 1986.

The $12,000 we spent on that Flotsam album was the biggest budget we'd invested in any record up to that point. We really wanted it to sound good because I believed those guys had the potential for a great future. It did extremely well.

When Metallica's Cliff Burton was tragically killed later that year, I got a call from Lars Ulrich. "Well, we need a bass player," he said sadly. It was just two weeks after Cliff had died. "Do you know anybody?" I had already thought about Armored Saint's Joey Vera until I heard he said he wasn't into it. When Lars asked the question, I immediately thought of Jason Newsted, who played with Flotsam and Jetsam. "I think I know the perfect guy for you," I told him.

Around the same time, Michael Alago—the A&R guy who signed Metallica to Elektra—had heard the Flotsam record and really liked it. Michael and I both sent the Metallica guys some stuff. "Yup, he sounds interesting," they said. "Can you put us in touch?" I said, "Sure, let me talk to him first and make sure he's into it."

I knew Jason was a huge Metallica fan, and when I called him he freaked out. But I could tell he was also in a weird position. Flotsam and Jetsam was his band; he wrote the songs and ran the whole thing. Even for me, it was a little bittersweet. Here was this great band that had just put out this great record. But the Metallica guys were good friends of mine, and clearly Jason was the perfect fit for them. I wanted the best for Jason and for Metallica, but I also knew I'd be losing something to make that happen.

"Give me a night to think about it," Jason told me. The next day he called me back and said he was in. He was the second bass player I'd recruited for Metallica, but I made a point of telling him exactly how things were likely to go. After all, he was a young, twenty-three-year-old kid. Jason was really smart, but I knew that the transition wasn't going to be an easy one for him. He was going from a band where he controlled everything to Metallica, where he would have zero control over anything. I vividly remember saying, "You've got to be aware that this band belongs to James and Lars, and you will have no say in anything. You're just going to be the bass player, and you're going to have to be OK with that. You probably won't get to contribute anything, and you certainly won't have any input in terms of the band's direction. You're just going to get up on stage and play bass."

He was fine with it at the start, but I know one of the main reasons he left fifteen years later—apart from the fact that he was a wreck, physically—was that he missed being able to write his own music and do his own thing. He wanted to control his own destiny, but what a great run and a great career the guy had.

Hooking them up with Jason signaled the end of my formal relationship with Metallica. We've always remained close friends and they've always been incredibly appreciative of the role Metal Blade played in terms of putting them on the map. Pretty much every time I see James he says, "Thank you so much for giving us the start. If it wasn't for you…"

When Metallica released *Master of Puppets* in 1986 and went on the road opening for Ozzy, you could tell they were going to be a monstrous band. It was then that the scene we were involved with caught up with what had been going on in Europe since 1984. It absolutely exploded. It was no longer a case of there being a bunch of struggling bands playing in their own private underground echo chamber. The metal scene had become something very significant. When it became obvious that Metallica was going to get huge, there was a sense that all of us were going to get swept up in the whole thing.

For an independent label, it was something of a double-edged sword. Yes, the movement was gathering pace, but as it did, bands that might previously have signed with an independent like Metal Blade were now attracting the attention of major labels. Despite that, we were starting to become what you'd call a legitimate company, with multiple employees and a bigger office on Sherman Way. I even moved out of my mom's house into an apartment after I woke up one day thinking, "I can't live at home *forever!*"

The employee who you could describe as the first major acquisition for Metal Blade was Jon Sutherland. Jon was a pretty renowned journalist in LA, where he started writing for a whole bunch of music magazines in the late seventies. I'd been reading his stuff for a long time, and we became friendly. When he started doing some promotional work for another label, I said, "Hey, Metal Blade's starting to do reasonably well and we don't have anyone doing publicity, per se. Could we hire you, here and there, on a case-by-case basis?"

Jon was into it, so we did a couple of collaborations that worked out really well. From there he ended up in our office, pretty much running our publicity staff for several years.

It was Jon who recommended another key staff member, Mike Faley.

Mike was managing Billy Sheehan, who he still manages to this day. Mike was from Buffalo. Billy, who was also from there, had moved to LA. What I needed at that point was someone to deal more directly with the bands, so Jon mentioned that he knew this guy, Mike Faley, who was trying to figure out a way of getting to LA.

Mike Faley (Metal Blade)

Billy and I went to grammar school together and, without a doubt, he is one of the greatest bass players of all time. He is the Hendrix or Van Halen of bass guitar. I had represented Billy while he was a member of a Buffalo band called Talas, and, in 1986, he had just joined the David Lee Roth Band. He wanted me to move to Los Angeles to be closer to him and the music industry generally. I reached out to people I knew in the business about looking for work in LA. One of those people, Jon Sutherland, was the press person at Metal Blade Records and also a writer who had done some great press pieces on Billy in the past. He mentioned me to Brian Slagel, and the first time I ever met Brian was on the phone. It took three phone calls, and the deal was done. The final deal point was that it was December in LA, and the sun was shining. I was in Buffalo, zero degrees and snowing. Sold!

Mike moved out to LA to help run the label, more or less, and has been here ever since. I'd been dealing with managers, booking agents, and so many bands while trying to run a business. It had become impossible, and Mike had a lot of connections. He already knew a lot of the agents and managers, so his skill set was exactly what I needed help with at exactly the right time. You could say Jon and Mike's arrivals signaled the beginning of a structured office framework, with designated people assigned to specific areas of the business. Meanwhile, William Berrol's career was taking off while he was still doing our legal work.

William Berrol

You always remember and value the relationships that started you on the path you wanted to be on. I wanted to be a music lawyer and have never done anything since. Brian is one of my most valued clients because his business is a mechanism by which I got an opportunity to learn much more than I knew about what it takes to run a label, to do a publishing deal, and to do an artist deal. It was beneficial for me from a financial point of view, but also from a learning perspective. And it was all done in an environment that was very innocent, but also very challenging. Even thirty-five years later, there's always something new.

Mike Faley (Metal Blade)

I was brought in as Label Manager in January, 1987. Each day provided me with new opportunities and challenges. My expertise was in touring and management, which brought a different, but much needed, perspective to what Metal Blade was doing. And being at a label gave me the opportunity to grow into a well-rounded music industry professional. I went from label manager to president of the label, but all our roles at Metal Blade were to help the artists achieve their potential without forcing the bands to change their identity. Brian and I had both seen the pitfalls of great bands signing to major labels, only to see them get watered down or have to sell out in order to appease the label.

My job has always involved liaising with managers, booking agents, artists, producers, and lawyers. Signing bands, marketing, soliciting artists to managers and agents, securing endorsements, and marketing partners suited to the artist's credibility are all part of the job. At Metal Blade, we all wear many hats, and that allows us all to work that much better for an artist. One of the bigger challenges that never seems to change is the need to fix problems. My motto is, "There are no problems, just solutions." The skill is in finding the right solution that works.

While pieces of our business framework were falling into place, I still wasn't getting up every day trying to find a way to make millions of dollars. I was putting out records (the *Metal Massacre* compilation series continued on a roughly yearly basis, in addition to the many albums we released each year), helping out musicians, and enjoying being a fan.

With that dual relationship comes a fine tightrope to walk. You want to do things from a fan's perspective, while remembering that, fundamentally, you *are* running a business. No matter how you feel emotionally, the numbers have to work. And sometimes it can be difficult to make decisions that you really don't want to make. Sometimes you might have to tell friends something they don't want to hear, or there might be a situation where they want something that you just can't do or don't think is right. It's a tricky situation, but I kept learning as I went along.

Having said all that, the financial side isn't the primary consideration when it comes to signing a band. If I love it, I'll do it—and then I'll own the consequences. There have been a lot of bands that we've thrown a ton of money at only for it not to work out, and we ended up losing money. But, really, I don't care. They were still great records, and we gave the bands a shot. You can't cry over spilled milk, and that's one of the reasons I've lasted so long in the business. Mistakes will happen, but it's how you deal with them that matters more than anything.

William Berrol

I literally still have a conversation with Brian every day where I say, "You're making a decision for the art, and the commerce is suffering here." And he always says, "Yeah, that's fine." And that's where I'm always profoundly struck by what the motivation is for the direction of Metal Blade. If you make decisions solely based on business, all too often, you'll subjugate the art. He's constantly doing things to expose music that he feels should have a voice, rather than constantly exposing music that he thinks will make him and his company more money. Money and economics always come second at Metal Blade.

✻

Speaking of making mistakes running a company, I made a continuing one from late 1987 through 1989 that could have resulted in me losing the company. I was always a huge vinyl fan, given that I'd started out in the business importing and buying vinyl. When CDs gradually started appearing, everyone was saying that vinyl was going to go away. I refused to believe that, to the extent that I told anyone who'd listen, "It's categorically not going to happen. It's impossible."

Metal Blade, unlike a lot of other companies, didn't really stop manufacturing vinyl. If you look at the release schedule, I don't think we ever put out more records than we did in the late eighties, which was right in the midst of that transitional time in the industry. We kept making vinyl and kept selling it, but one day—I can't recall exactly when—I got a phone call from our distributor, Greenworld. "By the way," they told me, "we've got a massive return coming back to you."

I'll never forget the awful feeling I had when I heard that. The color drained from my face. It turned out all the stores had decided vinyl was over and that compact discs were the new thing. It *felt* like they all made that decision on the same day. And, with that, the retail outlets were shipping huge quantities of vinyl back to the distributor. Our stock was essentially out on consignment, and so much of it came back that there was literally no more money. It was a landslide of the most immense proportions. We were on the hook for everything! The frustrating thing was that it had nothing to do with the actual music; it was simply because stores had decided the vinyl medium was extinct.

Consequently, there was a time frame of roughly six months where there was absolutely no money coming into Metal Blade. But we still had staff to pay, records to keep making, and bills to settle. The only way I could survive was to fund the company on the fifteen credit cards I went out and applied for. What's funny is that I used to get annoyed by getting those credit card applications through the door. For years, I didn't want them. Now I wanted *all* of them. And that's the only reason we survived.

We'd hit a brick wall where I owed money to the distributor, but had no money coming in and didn't know if I ever would again. In retrospect, had I listened to everyone's warnings about manufacturing too much vinyl, it might have all been different. Instead, my nostalgic side took over. I kept telling myself, "No, no, I love vinyl. Vinyl will never go away—too many people love it!" It was pretty bleak, and all those records coming back was the closest I ever came to just saying, "That's it. It's over." But I ultimately decided that we were absolutely going to keep on going and try to turn the situation around. I just couldn't quit.

The only smart thing I did in that era was that I kept all the vinyl in our manufacturing warehouse. People used to periodically say, "Should we get rid of some of this stuff?" But I could never part with it. Even when vinyl was stone dead, we had a gigantic wall of it in our warehouse. Thankfully, it all worked out eventually. When vinyl came back into fashion, we had massive quantities. We eventually sold all of it. It just didn't happen until more than twenty years later!

For a good portion of that period, we were barely hanging on. We didn't put out a huge number of records at the time. One album of note that did come out that year was Lizzy Borden's *Visual Lies.* It was something of a turning point in that it was the first time we'd gone out looking for a big-name producer. Max Norman had done Ozzy's first five solo records (and would later produce Megadeth's *Countdown to Extinction* and *Youthanasia,* among many others). He was a huge producer in heavy music, with a state-of-the-art studio up in Massachusetts.

We were all fans of everything Max had done, and I had some connections with him through his management. We sent him all the music to see if he was into it. With producers like Max, there are a few criteria. Number one, he has to want to do it. Then there's the discussion about budget, timescale, and location. Max loved to work in his home studio. I'd actually been up there in the past with the guys from Concrete Marketing, who would later manage Pantera and White Zombie. It was the first time I'd ever gone anywhere in a private jet and, when we landed, there were several feet of snow on the ground. We looked around the studio, and it was amazing. I was thinking, "It would be great to do something here one day."

As it turned out, Max was into Lizzy's album. We managed to negotiate a really favorable rate, although we still had to pay Max what he needed. All in all, it was an amazing experience to be able to work with such a revered name in the metal world with a big budget, in a great studio. The album turned out to be phenomenal. It was arguably Lizzy's biggest record.

Lizzy Borden

LA in 1987 was the epicenter of the metal movement. At the time we didn't realize it; we thought it would go on forever and keep getting bigger and bigger. But for that album, I knew where we needed to be. I dropped everything and said, "We're not going to record albums like we did before. We're going to write songs, not musical productions." I saw what was happening out there. The path forward was there for me to get my songs heard all around the world, but to do it, I knew I had to hire a producer. That was the first step. It wasn't me keeping up with the Joneses; we were just taking the next step as a big fish in the pond. We were one of the number one bands in all of LA; every show was sold out. So we had to go somewhere further, and the only way was to make a good record that would compete with other bands. Even though we were on a small label, I never thought we were a lesser band.

We occasionally hired outside producers, or, in the case of bands that were located far away from LA, producers located near the group's home base (Nasty Savage's *Indulgence* in Florida and Hallows Eve's *Tales of Terror* in Atlanta, for example). But we were still using Bill Metoyer and Track Record studio as much as we could. If possible, we'd get the bands to travel to LA for that purpose.

I look back on 1988 with amazement in terms of how many releases we put out. It was by far the most we'd ever attempted: Candlemass, D.R.I., Nasty Savage, Fates Warning, Armored Saint, Sacred Reich, Cryptic Slaughter—the list is long. It was a crazy time for us, but this was the time period when a few bands started leaving the label. In some ways that was a good thing because it brought us some welcome attention, but, on the other hand, you don't want to be losing bands from the roster. I think we lost twelve or thirteen bands to major labels in the period between 1988 and 1989 alone.

As time passed, we started to notice that some of these groups weren't doing as well at their new label as everyone expected. We thought if we could somehow align ourselves with a major, we could come up with an agreement where they could do the distribution, and we could keep the bands in house instead of losing them. The idea gained steam when our distributor suddenly went bankrupt.

As Greenworld, our original distributor, got bigger through the mid-eighties, they decided they wanted to form a label, in addition to their distribution arm. That's what they did in 1984 when they created Enigma Records. As time went on, they also forged a partnership with Capitol Records. We, in turn—in a roundabout way—did some stuff with Capitol Records, too. But all of it ended in disaster.

Enigma had a lot of success with bands like Poison, whose 1986 record *Look What the Cat Dragged In* sold tons and tons of copies. They were working with Capitol Records, so, at some point, Capitol bought half of Enigma, which obviously strengthened that relationship further. Unfortunately for us, while that relationship developed, Greenworld started paying less attention to us and other labels they were supposed to be distributing. Their focus was definitely elsewhere. And, because they'd had some success, they started to think that pretty much every band they signed was going to become a massive triumph.

The situation was made more awkward by the fact that I was friendly with the people at Capitol, since we'd used the studio for years to record and master some of our releases. My relationship with Capitol put a strain on my existing relationship with Enigma. The Greenworld staffers would tell me, "You shouldn't be dealing with people at Capitol. It all has to come through us."

Everything started to get really uncomfortable until, in late 1988 or early 1989, the half of Enigma that Capitol hadn't bought went bankrupt. It was the classic case of an independent label getting really big really fast. They end up thinking they know everything about what they're doing, and spending money like a major label when they don't have the catalogue to do so. When they went out of business, it was a massive problem, because they owed us a lot of money. Since they *had* no money, we were forced to sue them. There was a six-month period of time when it was really ugly. To make matters worse, there was no money coming in.

While less cataclysmic than when the vinyl returns came back, this was another opportunity for me to break out the fifteen credit cards to keep the business afloat until the cash flow issues were resolved. This time, however, we knew we'd probably be OK. We had already begun talking to major labels with a view to some kind of a coalition, and that was beginning to take shape.

That whole era of interacting with major labels was a very surreal time for me. I was talking to Columbia and Warner Bros., the two biggest record companies that existed back then. They were massive rivals who seemed to spend a lot of time trying to one-up each other. There I was getting flown first class to New York to meet with the boss of Columbia. Then I'd be having meetings in LA with Mo Ostin at Warner Bros. He was one of the most recognizable figures in the business, having founded the label and signed Hendrix, Van Halen, and Frank Zappa, among others.

Just meeting these people was blowing my mind, but the fact that I was in business conversations with them, and that they both really wanted Metal Blade, was just crazy to me. It was the ultimate feeling of legitimacy after all the years of working on my own to build the business from the ground up. Suddenly, I was in a great position as the boss of, by far, the largest of the independent metal labels at the time. Not just that, but we'd had so many bands (like Slayer and Metallica) graduate from us to one of the majors that I'm sure these label executives thought, "These Metal Blade guys must know what they're doing."

I thought it was funny that, because of the strong rivalry at the time, they'd each ask what the other was doing. "What is Columbia saying?" they'd ask me at Warner Bros. "What did Warner Bros. tell you?" the Columbia people would want to know. I was sitting there in the middle. At some point, I was going to have to make a decision about which one of these giants I was going to side with. And I would need to make up my mind sooner rather than later because of the whole Enigma fiasco!

I ultimately chose Warner Bros. because—while they were still a major label—they were also an independent company. That aspect appealed to me, as did the fact that they were located in LA instead of New York. Even though it was 1989 and it was getting a little easier to connect with people, there was still a degree of comfort knowing that their office was just down the street, rather than all the way across the country.

I say that, but we actually *had* opened up an office in New York in 1989. I'd become very friendly with the guys at Concrete

Marketing, Walter O'Brien and Bob Chiappardi. I loved New York, and there was a great scene there. I felt that, in order to increase our viability, we really needed a presence on the East Coast. We started out with an office in Concrete's mailroom, where we had two desks. It grew from there to become a valuable satellite office with great proximity to the student radio scene and important conventions like CMJ.

I should say that the hardest meeting I ever had was when I had to go and meet with Don Ienner at Columbia to tell him that I was signing with his biggest rival, Warner Bros. He was understanding, and wished me the best of luck. Then, right afterwards, they did a deal with Earache because they couldn't get us. They wanted a metal presence that much!

Chapter 7
A MAJOR ALLIANCE

Needless to say, partnering with Warner Bros. quickly relieved our short-term financial problems. The Enigma debts were erased overnight, and there was more upfront capital available immediately. That said, getting more money up front wasn't necessarily a deal-clincher for me. I've never been a guy who wanted a lot of money—or a lot of advance money, in this case—because I know that, somehow, you've always got to pay it all back. I don't like having obligations hanging over my head.

Nevertheless, the mechanics of the deal with Warner Bros. meant an influx of money to Metal Blade that was available to spend on our bands. We not only had to spend a lot of money to make really good records—we also had to invest money in videos, since that was the time when MTV was growing and *Headbanger's Ball* had really started to take off. Metal was a nationwide phenomenon that everybody listened to. If you lived in Tulsa, Oklahoma in 1990, for example, MTV was the only way you were ever going to hear this stuff!

It was money we couldn't afford not to spend. *Headbanger's Ball* was the holy grail, in terms of the kind of exposure we were looking to get for our bands. If you had a video on the show, you were more or less guaranteed to sell records. Without one, bands were simply lost in a sea of competition. In the absence of any real radio support, making videos was something we had to stumble into. We'd made a few crude videos on a shoestring budget prior to the Warner deal, but now that we were affiliated with a major label, it demanded a higher standard.

There were other deal components that came into play with our Warner Bros. agreement, as well. As the major labels became more immersed in the heavy metal world during the late 1980s and into 1990, they gradually realized they didn't really have the support staff to properly work the material. Companies like Concrete Marketing stepped up and did a great job, but they couldn't do everything. We'd been helping a few of the labels by doing bits and pieces of marketing here and there. When it came to signing the Warner deal, that marketing angle had become really important.

The first level of our Warner deal was straight distribution for most of our material. Then there was a secondary level where they would assist with some of the marketing and promotion. Additionally, if we felt that something really had a chance to happen, it could become a full Warner Bros. and Metal Blade joint venture. Another interesting component of the relationship was that we would also function as a marketing arm for Warner Bros., since they had almost no metal people working for them. "You don't have a lot of metal," we told them, "but you clearly have a *few* things. We'd love to be able to help you out with it."

There was yet another element to the arrangement where they allowed us to go into their catalogue to mine material that wasn't otherwise available. At that point, a lot of their older stuff wasn't available on CD. Back then, a lot of the catalog CD projects that labels *were* releasing came with very basic packaging, often a two-page booklet and nothing else. This was long before the time when special features like bonus tracks and deluxe packaging became part of the reissue world. But we saw the opportunity to do more with enhanced artwork and improved sound.

We knew in advance that Warner Bros. had all these resources, and that part of the deal was a dream come true for me. We ended up doing five Thin Lizzy albums, three Alice Cooper records, and three Deep Purple releases. None of these had been available digitally simply because, as CD sales skyrocketed, the label just didn't have the time or know-how to go back and redo it all. It was really a gold mine!

We had previously dabbled in the world of reissues to some degree. We'd done a bit of the Ian Gillan material and a few other things, all of which had ended up selling extremely well. I think that's why Warner Bros. was willing to give us the space to reissue whatever we wanted. Being allowed into the vaults to look for master tapes of some of my favorite bands of all time was surreal. I was like a kid in a candy store.

Sometime back in 1986, Jon Sutherland was scheduled to do an interview with Alice Cooper prior to the release of his *Constrictor* record. Jon was a fan, but he knew I was a bigger fan. "You know *way* more," he told me. "Do you want to come and help me?" I didn't hesitate for a second. "Fuck yeah!"

As it happened, I knew Brian Nelson, Alice's long-time assistant, from my tape trading days at the Capitol Records swap meets. Brian and I would both be there looking for Alice Cooper records. He became such a big fan that Alice eventually ended up hiring him!

Jon and I went to do an interview that was supposed to last thirty minutes, but ended up lasting more than an hour. Alice kept saying, "No, don't let them leave!" Then, three or four months later, I was in Europe for some of the festivals. I went to see Lizzy Borden play the Reading Festival in England. Alice was there, too. It turned out that they were having an album release party for *Constrictor* shortly afterward. When I got to the party early, I sat down on a couch to chill for a moment. Just then, I felt someone tap me on the shoulder. "Hey Brian, how's it going?" It was Alice. I almost fell on the floor. I'd met him for an hour, and now he *knew* me!

When it came to doing the Alice Cooper reissues, I reached out to his people and told them we'd love to have some kind of involvement from Alice. They were very receptive to the idea. "Just let us know what you want him to do," they told me. Not only were we re-releasing the music, but we were also tweaking the packaging with new photos and liner notes. We got a bunch of stuff from Brian Nelson that was really helpful. Then I had the idea for Alice to handwrite a couple of paragraphs about each record that would be included in all the CD cases. He did, and I still have the originals in our office.

One of Alice's albums, *Muscle of Love*, was just fifty thousand copies away from being certified as a gold album. With the copies we sold with the reissue package, we actually reached that target. It was *kind of* like a Metal Blade gold record, and presenting Alice with the award was a personal highlight.

While we were in the Warner vaults researching the Alice releases, we found some two-inch tape reels of some of his live shows. I pulled the boxes off the shelf, muttering to myself, "What the fuck is this?" It turned out to be two shows from the *Billion Dollar Babies* tour in 1973. One was recorded in Dallas, and the other in Houston. It was like discovering a species that was thought to be extinct!

Bill Metoyer and I took the tapes to Track Record and couldn't believe what we were hearing—two unbelievable Alice Cooper shows recorded in perfect quality. We mixed them down a little, and excitedly approached his people: "Look what we found! We should do something with this!" They were hesitant. Alice didn't really like the shows, and there was a lot of stuff going on with the band at the time, so nothing happened. Later, when the *Billion Dollar Babies* reissue came out, I was pleased to see that they used a bunch of that live stuff as part of the bonus material. Nobody even knew this stuff existed until we found it in the vaults!

The Thin Lizzy process was similarly amazing. Before re-issuing their material, we remastered it. I was able to be in Capitol Studios with Eddie Schreyer while he did it. The Lizzy remasters were something I was particularly happy about. I'd always felt that the quality of the originals was not as good as it could have been, but we actually had the original tapes to work with. We spent a *lot* of time on them, with complete attention to detail. It was well worth it. Philomena, the late Phil Lynott's mom, has been quoted as saying that they are the best quality. Scott Gorham, one of Thin Lizzy's guitar players, said the same thing.

Some of the recordings have been reissued again since we lost the rights, but it's gratifying to know that they've always wanted to use our masters. It's humbling to have had the opportunity to be involved with these legendary recordings—to even have had the original four-inch tapes of *Black Rose* in my hands. Incidentally, when we started mastering it, the tape started falling apart. I was about to have a heart attack until Eddie said, "Don't worry. When tapes are very old, you have to put them through a low-temperature baking process to get rid of the moisture and preserve them." The thought of putting tapes in an oven sounded wild at the time, but I soon learned it's a time-tested method for audio engineers. Once we did that, everything was fine.

Warner Bros. was extremely helpful when it came to working out royalties for the Thin Lizzy material because there was a pretty sizeable balance that the band had never recouped. Initially the estate was a little reluctant, saying, "Well, there's not much in it for us." But then Warner Bros. stepped up and said, "We'll wipe out the whole debt and pay you from the first unit of these reissues." With that, the estate was in! That was a generous a gesture on Warner Bros.' part.

With all of the reissues, there was a satisfying sense that events had come full circle. I was the kid scrounging around swap meets for Alice Cooper records—the kid whose musical life was turned upside down by one spin of *Machine Head*. And there I was, many years later, actually involved with the original recordings and, in a sense, the preservation of a movement I'd fought so hard to bring to people's attention. It was all very gratifying.

With the rising dominance of CDs, there was a period of time when it seemed that endless opportunities for reissues were up for grabs. We saw that potential and scheduled meetings with *everybody* with a view to revisiting out-of-print recordings. As a result, we managed to negotiate reissuing all the Starz stuff, as well as Earl Slick's material. This was all great stuff from the seventies that I *loved*. We had a million meetings with the Angel people, but, at the last minute, the label suddenly decided, "If they want to do it so much, why shouldn't *we* just do it?" It was a fair point. Eventually a lot of other labels just started doing it themselves, too, which was fine by me. At least the music was getting released!

⁂

As the 1990s approached, things were starting to change. I had become really good friends with one of Capitol's A&R people around 1988, which was prior to our alliance with Warner Bros. We were trying to find something to work on together, which culminated in us flying up to Seattle to check out a band called Mother Love Bone.

The group, which hadn't even been signed when we saw them play, was basically the forerunner of the band that would become Pearl Jam. They were fronted by singer Andrew Wood, who should have become a massive star, but ended up overdosing on heroin in early 1990. We saw them play in a bar in Belltown with maybe a hundred people packed around a tiny stage. The late Kurt Cobain and the late Chris Cornell were amazingly talented legends, but forget *any* of those now-iconic lead singers from that scene; Andrew Wood was a *rock star*. He was unbelievable. We were freaking out, and could see that something new was coming.

As much as I love metal, I would grow to love the Seattle scene, too. It was so fresh, and it made complete sense that it was going to absolutely kill anything that was going on with heavy metal at the time. My attitude was, "OK, it's going to happen. Let's get in at the beginning."

In retrospect, I think that approach really helped us navigate the tricky years ahead. The music itself was still metal; all these guys were hugely influenced by it, but not one of them would acknowledge it. Metal, in many people's minds, had become a caricature of itself and wasn't to be taken seriously. The bands that were part of the grunge scene earned a certain level of legitimacy by distancing themselves from metal.

For example, Alice in Chains' Layne Staley—who was one of the loveliest guys you could ever meet—was a monster metalhead. Strangely, he always reminded me of John Bush. Funny enough, a video appeared on YouTube years later of Layne's high school band covering some Armored Saint songs. My friend Nick Terzo ended up signing Alice in Chains. Just after he did, he sent me their demo and asked what I thought. When I'd listened to it, I called him back immediately. "Holy fuck," I shouted. "This is insane!"

Metal Blade was involved from day one with all the marketing efforts for Alice in Chains (and, for that matter, with Mother Love Bone's short run, up until the tragic death of Andrew Wood). I saw AIC's first LA show in front of maybe eight people. Then, in 1991—when they were brought in to replace Death Angel on the revolving Clash of the Titans tour—things really started taking off for them. I remember being up in Toronto recording *Parallels* with Fates Warning when that tour came through town. We all ended up going to the show together. When we were hanging out backstage, Layne came up and whispered in my ear, "Would it be OK if I got an autograph from the Fates Warning guys? I'm a huge fan!" I told him they'd be honored, but it was funny how he felt he had to be quiet about it!

Despite the shift in the metal scene, Alice in Chains didn't *always* go over well with audiences during the Clash of the Titans tour. Slayer fans aren't known to be the most tolerant to new bands. When you add Megadeth and Anthrax into the mix, it doesn't get any easier. Regardless, Alice in Chains— and grunge generally—was going to explode no matter what happened. Obviously, because of the metal stigma, none of those Seattle bands could ever sign with Metal Blade. Instead, we were satisfied to be involved on the marketing and promotion end. We were glad to at least be in the movement on some level.

Similarly, we helped Faith No More's "Epic" get huge rotation on MTV. Their album, *The Real Thing*, was one of the first records that came out during our partnership with Warner Bros. I was immediately a monstrous fan, and literally begged Warner's to let us work it. Luckily, I knew the band's manager pretty well, so they gave us the go-ahead.

We got into it full-on. Nobody really knew what this band was and, for a while, nobody *wanted* to know. This was the era when acts were categorized so tightly that if you liked Slayer, for example, you couldn't also like Queensrÿche. And if you liked Queensrÿche, you couldn't like whatever other hard band someone might be into. Everything was very rigid, so the diehard metal fans weren't into hearing about Faith No More.

Gradually a buzz started to build because nobody could deny that *The Real Thing* was actually a great *metal* record. It crossed so many boundaries at the same time. We kept pushing and pushing until one of our friends, Rick Krimm, who was in charge of programming at MTV, got hold of it. I was on him constantly. "You *have* to add Faith No More," I'd tell him. "They are going to be huge." Initially, because the album was a slow burn that took maybe eight months to catch fire, he'd say "I can't do it yet," Brian. "I just can't do it *yet*."

Then, one day I got a call from Rick saying, "Hey, I've got good news for you. I'm going to add 'Epic' into heavy rotation on MTV." And the rest is history.

※

Even with our behind-the-scenes involvement with the birth of grunge, as well as the Warner Bros. connection, Metal Blade was always primarily focused on discovering new bands and exposing new talent. Because we still had the Death Records label for all the punk and alternative releases, we were still receptive to anything that was great—even if it may not have necessarily fit precisely on the main metal-focused label. We'd become aware of a band called Goo Goo Dolls via Mike Faley's connections in Buffalo. William Howell, who helped out with A&R during the late eighties, had heard their self-titled debut, and it was he who suggested we might want to sign them to Death Records.

At that point, Goo Goo Dolls was very definitely a *punk* band. Yes, they had some metal overtones because of how the songs were structured, but, at the heart of it, they were a three-piece punk outfit. Regardless of how you'd categorize them, they were a really fun band, and were amazing in a live setting.

We did two records with them prior to the Warner deal—*Jed*, in 1989, followed by *Hold Me Up* a year later. Things were getting better and better for them, and we really felt they had potential for a much bigger level of exposure than where they were. Everything was there for them, and we kept feeling like they were always on the brink of the next level. But it took a lot longer than we thought it would. Then, when the Warner Bros. relationship happened, those guys definitely had Goo Goo Dolls on their radar. Indeed, one of the first things we thought, prior to getting together with Warner Bros., was that the band would be a perfect fit for that relationship.

Superstar Car Wash, released in 1993 and distributed by Warner Bros., did well. People loved it; critics reviewed it positively, and it got very, very close. But, in the end, it didn't quite reach the levels we thought it should have. That was a surprise to me, because Goo Goo Dolls represented exactly what was happening at that time. They were a great alternative band. It was one of those situations where, for whatever reason, things just didn't happen for them like they should have. We kept trying because we loved them. They were still selling a lot of records and doing a lot of touring. We weren't going to give up, but it was getting to the point where the guys weren't totally sure what they were going to do long term. Johnny Rzeznik was taking bartending lessons while Robby, the bass player, started getting more involved in the studios in Buffalo. I think they were keeping their options open in case the music career didn't work out.

�֎

A couple of years later, after we'd made the official separation from Warner Bros., they were making the next record, which would become 1995's *A Boy Named Goo*. Johnny came to me with a song called "Name." We'd always had a good relationship during the recording process. I'd listen to the demos and give them feedback on the songs. It was very healthy; we all just wanted to make sure they were putting the right material out there. While Warner Bros. would distribute the album as part of our separation agreement's terms, it remained a Metal Blade release.

"Name" was a little bit out of the ordinary. While they had touched on acoustic music, they were still, fundamentally, a rock band. The song was almost a last-minute afterthought. "Should I put this on the record?" Johnny asked me.

"Yeah, let's do it," I said. The song had already been recorded, so it didn't make sense to waste it.

When the record came out, we were working it the way we normally worked new albums. Goo Goo Dolls got a little radio success with the first couple of songs and then, one day, Kevin Weatherly, who was the Program Director at KROQ in Los Angeles, caught wind of it. Kevin was the top guy in LA, and when he found something he loved, he wouldn't let it go. He's the guy who broke Red Hot Chili Peppers and pretty much every band from that early nineties LA scene. A radio programmer carried a lot of influence back then.

One night he put "Name" on the radio just to see what would happen, and people went crazy. Within a couple of days, the song was on heavy rotation on KROQ and absolutely exploding. Meanwhile, we were already working on the video for the next single. We stopped, dropped everything else, and focused on "Name." From there, Goo Goo Dolls took off and became an overnight sensation. Obviously they had an existing platform and people knew who they were, but they went from selling a couple of hundred thousand albums to selling Gold records in a matter of weeks.

�֎

Another band we became aware of in 1989 was Cannibal Corpse, which, like Goo Goo Dolls, originated in Buffalo. One of the local promoters there sent Mike Faley a tape and encouraged us to check it out. He brought the demo tape into the office and, when I looked at the cover, I noticed there was a song called "A Skull Full of Maggots." I looked at Faley. "I don't care what it sounds like," I told him. "We *have* to sign them." I put the tape in anyway, just to be sure, and it was *amazing*.

Chris Barnes (Cannibal Corpse and Six Feet Under)

After my band Leviathan ended, I started Cannibal Corpse with Paul and Bob, and then Jack and Alex got in the band. I was working at Cavages record store, doing warehouse work, and I met the main buyer for the chain. John Grandoni was his name, and he became a very good friend of mine. He was also friends with Mike Faley at Metal Blade, and he guided me through the basics of the music industry. He said, "Chris, I know you have a band, and I know this guy at Metal Blade records. I can send a press package, but here's what you need: a video of you guys playing live, a biography, and a demo tape."

He sent the package in and then, at the end of July of 1989, John called me. "Chris, come over," he said. "I've got something to show you." He handed me a package that had a record contract in it and a letter saying that they'd like to offer us a seven-album deal. It was a big honor, and quite surreal. Here was the record label that I loved so much growing up, and they thought our band was good enough to sign. I was blown away. It felt like I was living in a movie. Right from the beginning, we had a pleasant experience. Everyone felt like a friend, and it has never changed.

An Interview with Alex Webster
of Cannibal Corpse

What scene, if any, existed in the Northeast in the late eighties? Were you the only band playing the kind of music you played?

There was a good underground scene in Western New York (Buffalo and Rochester), which is the area we are from. We definitely weren't the only band that was playing thrash or death metal there in the late eighties, and, in fact, all of us had already been in other bands before we formed Cannibal Corpse.

Where did the motivation for such extreme music, in tandem with gory lyrics, come from?

Like a lot of the bands and metal fans we knew at that time, we enjoyed horror movies. Some of the lyrical ideas had to have come from that source. Additionally, the bands we listened to in those early days (like Slayer, Death, Kreator, Sodom, and so on) had dark and violent lyrics. So, really, the idea of combining extreme music and lyrics was already there. Our band's style was sort of an extension of the bands we liked. I think that's how it is for a lot of bands; you expand on your influences, and you end up creating your own style. Obviously, in our case, we tried to up the ante in terms of musical speed and lyrical violence. The result of our efforts was the Cannibal Corpse style of death metal.

Did you find the term "death metal" limiting, or did it give you an identity and a genre?

We were and still are quite proud to be called death metal, and we're always happy to work within the constraints of the genre. There's a lot of room for creativity within the boundaries we've set for ourselves. All the members of Cannibal Corpse listen to all sorts of different music, but we're adamant about making our band's music full-on death metal. If any of us have felt like stepping outside of those boundaries, we've done it in other projects. Cannibal Corpse is, and will always be, death metal.

What were the circumstances that brought your demo to Brian's attention? Did signing with Metal Blade seem like an obvious move? Was there interest from other labels at the time?

Our original singer, Chris Barnes, used to work at a record store in the Buffalo area, and his boss at the store, John Grandoni, was a friend of Mike Faley's. Mike is also originally from the Buffalo area and is essentially Brian's right-hand man at Metal Blade. Chris asked John if he could get our tape over to Mike, which he did, and, from there, Mike let Brian take a listen. They liked what they heard, and shortly thereafter we received a contract offer from them. It all happened pretty quickly, but clearly Brian and Mike heard potential and decided to give us a chance. We hadn't received any real interest from any other labels at that point, as far as I remember. In hindsight, I'm glad we didn't, because Metal Blade wound up being the perfect label for us. It's nice when the only choice you have is the right choice!

Has the resistance you've had to your music and imagery over the years—being banned in certain countries and at certain times—encouraged you to become even more extreme?

No, I don't think so. We've always done what we felt was right for our songs, period. We wouldn't let outside forces influence our artistic direction.

In general, has Metal Blade always been supportive of what you do? How much input did/does Brian have? Have there ever been disagreements about the direction of the band?

Metal Blade has been extremely supportive throughout our career. Brian and everyone at the label have always stayed out of our way and let us do our music the way we want to do it. I don't remember any serious disagreements about direction, but we've made a few professional moves that the label may have initially questioned. The main one was our dismissal of our first singer, Chris Barnes. I'd say it's pretty reasonable for them to have questioned that move, but in the end, it worked out better for all parties.

Brian is as much a fan as he is a CEO. What do you see as his main strengths as a label boss?

Even beyond being a fan, Brian is a true metal expert. The decisions he makes as a boss are made from a very informed opinion on the music. Brian obviously has great business sense—Metal Blade's enduring success is a testament to that—but I do think he's put business second and music first on many occasions. He'll release music he loves, whether or not it's an obvious moneymaker. This can result in commercial disappointment from time to time, but I think, in the long run, it has paid off. Brian's sincerity is clear to metal fans worldwide, and that translates to long-term loyalty and interest in Metal Blade Records.

Chapter 8
PUSHING THE ENVELOPE

When we first got together with Warner Bros., we kind of knew it might be tough to put *everything* through their distribution channels. When I looked at our roster, I could see there were a few bands that just might not make sense for such a mainstream company. Cannibal Corpse was definitely one of them.

To circumnavigate the issue, we negotiated a side deal with Important, which would later become Relativity and, finally, RED Distribution. That gave us an outlet so that edgier material, like the Cannibal Corpse catalogue, could be released through them. While we *may* have been able to distribute Cannibal Corpse through Warner, part of me felt like it would be cooler for a band like that to be handled by independent distribution anyway.

The timing for a band like Cannibal Corpse was good, as far as I was concerned. By 1990, the whole metal scene was becoming kind of weird. The hair metal movement was at the forefront, and I didn't want to get involved in any of that. Despite our status as an important metal label, we stayed far away from any of those bands. As such, death metal seemed like an appropriate antidote, though I have to admit I wasn't the biggest fan at the very beginning. I'd heard Morbid Angel and Obituary—all these bands that Roadrunner was signing—but, honestly, I always preferred the thrashier bands like Nasty Savage, which were emerging from the same area.

When I got the Cannibal Corpse demo, there was something different. Having grown up as a huge fan of Alice Cooper and KISS—bands that really pushed the envelope—discovering a group like Cannibal Corpse made it hard *not* to be captivated by their aura and imagery. Fortunately, the music was really great, too.

As time passed, I grew to like death metal much more than I did at the beginning. It's funny, because a lot of people my age aren't into it. So many people in their forties or fifties say to me, "I just can't get into it. I can't deal with the vocals." Part of me totally understands that; it's a whole different thing from traditional metal. But, for me, it works precisely because of how the evolution of metal unfolded. As music was getting progressively heavier, bands were finding it difficult to do anything heavier with the vocals. Then, when death metal vocals came in, everything changed. What could be heavier than crushingly heavy music with those guttural vocals?

Of course, if you trace the lineage, all of it goes back to the influence of early metal bands like Venom. In the end, Metal Blade signed a lot of death metal bands, even though we were a little late to that party. Labels like Roadrunner and Earache definitely got in there before we ever did. My initial resistance to the style was probably part of the underlying reason.

More significant was the fact that, while these bands started to emerge during 1988 and 1989, we were still in the midst of financial turmoil prior to signing the deal with Warner Bros. It probably wouldn't have been the smartest move to immediately go out and sign a bunch of death metal acts the moment we inked our deal with them. That wasn't going to make Warner Bros. overly happy. In some ways, we had to watch what we did.

As heavy as death metal is now, it seemed much heavier back then by virtue of its underground status. Mainstream people had no idea what to do with it. While Warner Bros. was selling into independent stores, they were also selling to the major retail chains. If you'd talked to Wal-Mart about carrying an album called *Eaten Back to Life* by a band named Cannibal Corpse in 1990, they'd have asked if you were crazy.

Chris Barnes (Six Feet Under and formerly of Cannibal Corpse)

Brian liked to play tricks on me in the studio. When I was recording my vocals for the album Tomb of the Mutilated, he showed up right in the middle of the session. When I came into the control room from the booth at Morrissound, everyone had a pale look on their face. No expression. I said, "What's going on?"

Brian had some of my lyrics in his hand. "Man, I can't put this out," he said in a deadpan voice. "You're going to have to change it."

Everyone was silent; you could have heard a pin drop. I said, "What do you mean?"

He said, "This is just too much. There's no way I'm putting this out." He was serious, and all my passion about my lyrics accelerated in my head.

I flew off the handle, saying, "Well, I'm fucking quitting. I'm out of here!"

Then everyone started laughing. Brian looked at me and said, "I'm just kidding."

※

Around the same time, somebody told me to check out a band called Gwar. "They run into the crowd," I was told. "They throw blood and meat at people!" Everyone thought this was something I'd be really into. I didn't manage to see them the first year I went to the CMJ music festival in New York, but I didn't dare miss them the second year. They were completely amazing; they had on their costumes and were doing all this crazy stuff on stage.

My first thought was, "Are they normal, or are they out of their fucking minds?!" I remember sitting around after the show, discussing with some friends and colleagues whether or not we should work with Gwar. "If they're all completely sane," I said, "I want to do it."

Brad Roberts AKA Jizmak Da Gusha (Gwar)

I grew up in Detroit in the sixties and seventies, where there was a lot of Motown and big band and classic rock. And then, when it got into the eighties, I started discovering punk rock.

Gwar was made up of a bunch of do-it-yourself punk musicians and artists from Virginia Commonwealth University. We were a lot more influenced by punk than we ever were by metal, but with the barbarian costumes and the look, it was obvious that it could work in the metal realm, too.

For the most part, early on, Gwar's mythos was that we were from outer space, unfrozen out of our arctic cave by the giant clouds of aerosol hairspray that all the big hair bands had released in the eighties. It had poked a hole in the ozone and thawed us, and we were out to destroy the music and those people. That was Gwar's plan, because we were so mad at being stuck on planet Earth when we woke up from our frozen slumbers. So, from that perspective, we were the anti-metal band. We would purposely write songs that we felt were making fun of metal, but still had enough juice to make people think, "Oh, that's kind of like a metal song." Everything we did was satirical and, while we get pigeonholed as a metal band, we started out as a punk band making fun of metal.

Surprisingly, when I met the Gwar guys later that evening, it turned out that they were all super normal college students from Virginia—guys with a lot of art and music in their backgrounds. Interestingly, in those days, the late Dave Brockie wasn't really the front man. Mike Bishop was the focus. They were a very different band in those formative years. They looked different, and the stage show was extremely primitive compared to what they're doing now. Nevertheless, it was obvious they were all amazingly smart guys, and, as time went on, that was only confirmed by how undeniably creative they became with their art. In some ways, Gwar was the reason that a band like Slipknot, with the costumes and the imagery being as important as the sound they made, was allowed to exist.

Brad Roberts

I'd gotten into the group in 1989, and then we recorded our second album, Scumdogs of the Universe—probably the most famous of all our records. We'd done it with a company from London called Master Records, which was owned by the singer from the old ska band Bad Manners. That record did fairly well, and then Metal Blade was interested in picking us up after that release. Being quite new to the band, I wasn't too involved in the discussions—the elder statesmen were pretty involved. I do remember that other labels were looking at us. My understanding then was that Metal Blade was an independent label, but kind of a subsidiary of Warner Bros. Records.

The stuff that Gwar was doing was insanely amazing—to the extent that, in retrospect, I think a lot of what they were doing on stage went over the heads of many of their audience members. There was a strong political element to their performance, but there were also plenty of other subjects they'd go on long satirical rants about, too. I absolutely loved it, but I don't think everybody got it. Regardless, they were brilliant, and continued to be for many years. What I didn't know when I signed them was that Gwar would have a significant impact in terms of Metal Blade's destiny in the upcoming era.

An Interview with Tracy Vera, Metal Blade CFO and GM

What were the circumstances by which you came to be employed by Metal Blade? What were your aspirations in life prior to that? I assume you were always a fan of this kind of music?

I'm a huge fan of many kinds of music in general, and am a child of hippie parents who were into the Velvet Underground, Cream, Hendrix, The Doors, The Rolling Stones, The Mothers of Invention, and Dylan. From that upbringing, it was just a short step to Black Sabbath, Rush,

The Scorpions, UFO, and then, a bit later, Judas Priest and Iron Maiden. During college (I have a master's in art and I still paint and show my work, but that's a whole other story), I started working at record stores in the early to mid-eighties in Connecticut, where I lived at that time. I eventually became the heavy metal buyer and, later, the head buyer of all music for the small chain.

Because everyone knew me from the store and knew that I was into metal, a local college station asked me to do a heavy metal radio show. All the students were so indie that no one wanted to do the metal show. I played all kinds of specialized metal at a time when the scene was just starting to bubble. Between the store and the radio show, I realized there was an actual music business, and I wanted to work in it more than anything else in the world. In 1990, I moved to Los Angeles and, through contacts I had made, got a job at Metal Blade doing retail marketing.

What would a typical day at Metal Blade (if there is such a thing) involve for you?

I think that's the thing I enjoy most about my job: it really isn't the same each day, and my job has evolved over time. It's still changing! Fridays, I meet with our lawyer to discuss legal issues or contracts we have pending; Wednesdays, we have a sales meeting to discuss what is happening worldwide that week in sales; and on Tuesdays, we have a staff meeting where we discuss marketing and releases. In between, I am responsible for the day-to-day operations and finances, so that takes up a good portion of time answering emails, creating and reviewing budgets and projections, scheduling releases, paying bills, reviewing contracts, and many more tasks.

I also get to travel quite often. For example, in May I went to London to meet with Sony, which recently purchased indie distributor Essential, to discuss whether it's the right thing for Metal Blade to move UK distribution from Sony to Essential. I'm the Managing Director of the European operation, so I travel to our office in Germany as often as possible to work with our wonderful staff there. I usually try to see our bands when I travel, as well. I love to pop up at shows around the world, and that is surely an opportunity not everyone has. It's great for getting a sense of the market and the audience for our music in other places. We want our perspective to remain broad.

How did you meet your husband, Joey, of Armored Saint and Fates Warning?

I remember one time I saw Joey come off the floor of the Palladium covered in Gwar fluid. It was the first time I went to see the band after I started at the label. Even though I had met him before, I really noticed him for the first time. My roommate said to me, "He's cute," and I thought, "There's my guy!"

Has it been easy working at the label, while your husband is a member of two of the label's flagship acts? Are there ever conflicts of interest?

Yes and no on conflicts of interest. In some ways, it's made it easier, and, in other ways, it's harder. Joey and I enjoy working together; we spend many evenings after dinner talking about work. I give him advice and perspective on how the business works in a general way. From him, I gain an understanding and sympathy for all recording artists, not just Armored Saint. He's also the point person for business, recording, and art for Armored Saint—as well as the label contact for the band—so we end up working together on that front. He's smart and I respect him, business-wise. I suspect he feels the same about me.

With Fates Warning, Jim Matheos is the primary contact, so I work with him. I've known him for years, even before I knew Joey. So, with Fates, there isn't any conflict between me and Joey. I think Joey and I have found a way to make it all work for the positive.

The way it is harder is that I am such an Armored Saint fan, but sometimes I have to take off my fan and wife hats, put on my work hat, and say, "Well, that budget is too high," or "That doesn't make sense." But honestly it doesn't happen very often because time has tempered both our expectations of how big a release is going to be or how many units it will sell. From a personal and business perspective, more would always be better, but at this point, I just think, "Did we do all we could as a label to help the band?" And Joey is thinking, "Is the release the best record it can be?" It's about a job well done on both our parts. He knows all the other people who work here pretty well, too, and that doesn't hurt Armored Saint, either. But is that a conflict? Metal Blade is all about the big family of staff and bands we have around the world.

What are Brian's main strengths?

He's great, and that's the main reason I've worked here since 1990. He's super generous and good to people. He's kind of a "rock star" in his own right, and can command a room. But Brian has great business instincts and a good head for numbers. He's also a people person. Our bands love him; he takes the time to hang out with them, and he's a genuine fan—and he's a big reason why bands stick with us so long. He also has great ears, both as a producer and in being able to hear the potential in a band.

If you could pick an experience in your time with the label that you've most enjoyed, what would it be?

I've been so lucky. There have been so many, but they often cross over between personal and business. Work is work, but I've gotten to have amazing experiences as a result of working at Metal Blade. Seeing Armored Saint play at the Metallica thirtieth anniversary show at the Fillmore was a huge highlight. That same night, King Diamond came out and performed, as well. And I got my photo taken with Lou Reed and Marianne Faithful! I love that photo. King hugged me right before I made Scott Ian take the photo and, if you look closely, I have an upside-down cross on my face from King's makeup. Wonderful!

Another time, Metal Blade had a party in Japan for the opening of our office there (which has since closed), and Unearth played on the same trip. Johan from Amon Amarth came on the trip, as well as a bunch of our staff. Joey came with me, and it was a great time doing beer bongs backstage and all kinds of shenanigans. We went out to eat afterwards. I ordered octopus, but when the dish was served, they were little fried baby octopi with tiny eyes looking up at me. I never forgot that. I ate them anyway, since I at least try to be adventurous. But it was a great trip. I always love Tokyo.

Going to Midem in Cannes in Provence, France, year after year, was quite an experience. Brian and I would go there to meet with all our distributors, or potential distributors, from around the world. Midem itself was often grueling, with ten or twelve hours of meetings a day for four days. But, in the evening, you go out for killer French food and wine. It's where my palate for wine was developed. I firmly blame Brian for my taste in wine, since he would always order great wine to accompany our meals there.

One of the most significant albums in Metal Blade's entire catalogue was Armored Saint's *Symbol of Salvation*, which was released in 1991, when they returned to the label. We had a long relationship with the band, and, despite the fact that they had gone on to sign with Chrysalis, we had always remained very good friends.

While the band was recording demos for an upcoming record, Dave Prichard, the original guitar player, was diagnosed with leukemia. Dave was the nicest guy in the world, as well as a phenomenal writer and guitarist. He was so underrated and never really got the juice that he should have had.

In 1990, when bone marrow transplants were in their very early stages of development, the only way to have a good chance of survival was to get an exact match from a family member. Dave was adopted, and never knew his biological parents. Despite a lot of research, a family member couldn't be found. They located a donor who was a relatively close match, but it didn't work out. Sadly, he passed away.

At that point, Armored Saint was at the end of the Chrysalis deal. With Dave's death and no label, they were at a major crossroads. I thought they were probably done, since they didn't *want* to continue. At some point, while they were still figuring out what to do after the Chrysalis deal ended—but before Dave died—they made some amazing demos that featured Dave's playing. When I heard the recordings, I was certain they were some of the best songs Armored Saint had ever written.

After the band had some time to reflect, I went to them. "Look," I said, "we can't *not* put these songs out. It wouldn't be fair to Dave.

It's some of his best work, and some of the *band*'s best work. Let's at least find a way to release them."

John Bush
It was certainly our destiny to return to Metal Blade, and we were fortunate that Brian welcomed us back with open arms. That led to Symbol of Salvation. *Would life have been different if we had never left Metal Blade in the first place? Who knows? Luckily, even when we were at Chrysalis, Brian remained a huge fan and supporter of the Saint.*

I could tell they were warming to the idea as we discussed it. There were a few options at that time, which seemed to come out of nowhere given that the band appeared to be finished. One option, of course, was for them to come back to us. We were still in partnership with Warner Bros., and Q Prime, the management company that looked after Metallica and several other bands, had heard the demos and liked them. All of that positivity resulted in Armored Saint officially getting back together to realize the huge potential the *Symbol of Salvation* demos clearly had.

We begged Dave Jerden, who I knew from working on promotion for Alice in Chains, to produce the album. "Would you do this as a favor to us," we asked, "and not charge us a zillion dollars?" Dave agreed, and the record turned out phenomenally well.

The most satisfying part of the process was that we were able to "fly in" a solo Dave had done on one of the demos so it could be included on the final record. That wasn't easy to do in those days. Pro-Tools makes it very easy to separate tracks and move them around now, but, back then, the process of trying to take the solo off one tape and transfer it to another, in exactly the right timing, was very difficult. Somehow we were able to do it, and Dave lives on through those songs.

The record came out and did extremely well in getting Armored Saint back on track. They did massive world tours, and it was a rebirth for them. I still love that record, because it involved taking something that was in danger of slipping away and reclaiming its former glory. It's one of the highlights of my career.

John Bush

Symbol *is the "phoenix rising" record for Saint. Dave informed us that he was sick during the writing of it. We had just been dropped by Chrysalis, and no other record companies seemed interested. Our future was in doubt. However, as is normally the case in turbulent times, artists step it up even more, so we were writing some killer, heartfelt songs.*

Then Dave passed. I was ready to blow it out. Gonzo and Joey, however, were determined to make a record with the songs we had. The only way to regroup was to reclaim our identity as the family we were. Jeff returned; Phil returned. Brian and Metal Blade were back, and we enlisted Dave Jerden to produce it. That is why the record has the vibe it does.

※

When we signed the Warner Bros. deal, it was an independent company. Not long after, however, they merged with Time, Inc. to become the Time Warner Corporation. The change in the ownership and company structure resulted in a more conservative climate.

The early 1990s also saw the culmination of what had been a decade-long witch hunt over lyrics, with heavy music coming under particular scrutiny by the organization known as the Parents Music Resource Center, or PMRC. Ozzy Osbourne ended up in court in 1986 when the lyrics of his song "Suicide Solution" were blamed for the suicide of a teenager. Similarly, Judas Priest was taken to court in Reno, Nevada in 1990 over their song "Better by You, Better than Me," which was also blamed for a suicide. In both cases, the charges were unproven, but the effect on the record industry was wide-ranging. Labels were becoming much more conservative in terms of what lyrics they were willing to allow their bands to release.

My feeling was that the whole PMRC movement actually backfired. All it did was shine a spotlight on a lot of artists who otherwise would not have found national attention. Lizzy Borden and a few of our other bands had songs listed on the activist group's shit list, but every single group they targeted—whether it was W.A.S.P., Twisted Sister, or Lizzy Borden—got massive exposure and did really well because of it.

We'd get letters at the office every once in a while—usually from someone in the Midwest—saying, "How could you put these things out?" Honestly, we paid no attention. The only thing we ended up having to do was apply the warning stickers on the album covers. And, again, that helped sales. People were specifically buying the records with the PMRC stickers. In some cases—like with Gwar and Cannibal Corpse—we had to offer two versions: the uncensored version and the "clean" one. The "clean" ones generally didn't sell.

In 1992, Time Warner released the self-titled debut record by Body Count, which was Ice T's band. There was a song called "Cop Killer" on that album, which immediately drew widespread condemnation from authorities and political figures for its incendiary content. The record, which was shipped out to stores in a plastic "body bag," was eventually removed from shelves. But not before Warner Bros.—perhaps as a last act of defiance and the defense of the right to free speech—had flooded the market with half a million copies.

"Cop Killer" was a huge national issue, and the eventual result was that Body Count had to leave the label. The group just did not sit well with Time Warner's increasingly conservative views. Thereafter—and this is where we were directly impacted—Time Warner employed designated watchdogs to look at every single release that went through the system. They wanted to make sure that everything—including the artwork and lyrics—was Time Warner approved.

The first or second album we gave them after all this controversy was a Gwar release called *This Toilet Earth*. Gwar was a pretty big band at the time. We had the catalogue through Warner Bros., and we'd put out a couple of successful albums already (*Scumdogs of the Universe* and *America Must Be Destroyed*). We'd made a movie, *Phallus in Wonderland*, which was nominated for a Grammy in 1992. Gwar was an undeniably major act, but those guys were always walking on the edge. That Grammy evening, for example, epitomized everything Gwar was about.

Back then, the Grammy ceremony was a very formal event. A black tie was obligatory; you certainly couldn't get away with wearing a t-shirt. But the members of Gwar decided they were going to walk down the red carpet in full costume. Everyone was freaking out. All the major news channels wanted to do a feature on them. Even as they were walking into the venue, however, I wasn't entirely certain they were going to be allowed in the door with those costumes on. I was standing nearby, unsure what was going to happen next, when someone asked the usher, "Can they come in?"

The older lady at the door said, "Well, they have tickets, so I guess they can!"

Once we turned the new Gwar album in to the label, I got a report from one of the product managers at Time Warner saying, "Err, yeah. So, if you guys are going to put this record out, you'll need to cut this, remove that, change these lyrics to this song…"

I said, "Wait a minute. What are you talking about?"

"We have this new policy here," he explained, "and we can't have this record come out as it stands." This presented not only a commercial issue, but also an artistic issue. At no point had I ever influenced any of our artists in terms of content. I'd given advice based on what was best for the band from a creative standpoint, but I had never turned around and flat-out said, "You *can't* do this."

I went to Mo Ostin, with whom I'd signed the Warner deal at the outset, to voice my concerns. In retrospect, it was a pretty ballsy move on my part, but I just told him straight out, "If this is the way it's going to be—that you're going to tell me that I have to direct artists about what lyrics and art they can and can't have—I can't do this anymore." To his immense credit, he said, "We agree; we don't like it either, but this is the way it is."

Lizzy Borden

From the start, whatever came out of your imagination—that's what Brian wanted. He never interfered with the vision of a band. You hear stories where a band has their direction influenced, with songwriters being brought in, to the degree that their outlook is completely changed in terms of what the band thought they were doing. Brian never did that. He said, "Whatever you have to offer, that's what I want." That's one of the many things I liked: there was no interference at all with the artist's creative growth.

It was ultimately decided that Metal Blade should be released from the Warner deal, with one proviso: Goo Goo Dolls stayed with Time Warner, while every other band was retained by us. All of that drama over a Gwar record! I felt there was always a big part of Gwar's Dave Brockie that wanted to test boundaries after the whole "Cop Killer" thing had happened. He wanted to really go crazy on some of the song lyrics, and we ended up putting it out with all the songs and all the lyrics without any interference. That got some interesting publicity for everyone involved!

Brad Roberts (Gwar)

Brian was always a big supporter of Gwar. He has always backed us, and you can't deny the man's tenacity. Gwar has always demanded complete artistic freedom, which Metal Blade, for the most part, gave us. They'd

*suggest potential producers and ask to listen to mixes now and again—
things like that.*

We recorded a song on This Toilet Earth *called "Baby Dick
Fuck." I believe Metal Blade was at a point where their distribution
contract with Time Warner was up for renewal. Time Warner came to
Metal Blade and said, "You have to take that song off the record or we're
not going to distribute it." Of course, being young and proud musicians,
we said, "Screw you. Who are you? We deal with Metal Blade, not Time
Warner." We thought that to take it off the record would be a slippery slope,
because then Time Warner would have thought, "Oh, Gwar is cool." And
then maybe they'd have taken us from Metal Blade altogether, elevated us
in the record industry, but then they would have told us what kind of songs
to write. We saw that coming, and we didn't want to do it. We wanted to
dictate our terms and our art. Brian went to bat for Gwar and said, "Screw
our distribution deal with Time Warner. We'll find another distributor."
And then they put out the record, with the song on it. That says everything
about what kind of label Metal Blade is.*

Gwar is one of those bands that almost became absolutely
huge. We were *so close* to making big movies with huge budgets,
but something would always happen to derail progress—whether
they had a manager involved that didn't quite understand things,
or some other barrier that prevented them getting to the next level.
But—even though they never had a record that singularly sold
a million copies—they have still sold a lot of records over a long
period of time. They are so well respected by so many people, and,
to this day, they are doing amazing stage shows. They have set a
really high bar for other bands.

※

In early 1993, Cannibal Corpse, which was enjoying a steadily
rising profile following the *Tomb of the Mutilated* album, was
approached to contribute a track to a movie called *Ace Ventura: Pet
Detective*. The band and I were both sent the script and, on first
reading, I have to confess I thought it was pretty terrible. "I don't

know," I told the guys. "This looks goofy." We knew the lead actor, Jim Carrey, was in the show *In Living Color,* and that the movie was going to be a mainstream comedy. The clash of cultures was glaring. An underground death metal band getting involved with a family comedy film definitely seemed way out of the ballpark for a band that dark and heavy. I couldn't decide whether people would think it was cool, or whether they'd just think the band was selling out. One thing was for sure: I didn't want fans to suddenly stop buying the records of one of our flagship bands in exchange for a five-minute appearance in a movie, and that was definitely a possibility.

But the band wanted to do it. We talked about it and, at the end of a lot of discussion, I finally said, "It can't hurt. If you guys want to do it, I'm not going to tell you not to." From a logistical point of view it would be easy, because they were in Tampa and the movie was filming in Miami. Apparently, the reason they were approached in the first place was that Jim Carrey was a massive Cannibal Corpse fan. He asked for them *specifically* and told the producers to research them and make contact.

Chris Barnes

I remember getting the call from Mike Faley and thinking, "Oh my god, I love that guy. He's hilarious." Paul and I watched Jim Carrey's standup quite often, so I was all for it. I didn't have a problem with it, but I think Alex did. He said, "I don't think we should do it." I thought it was a great opportunity for us. We all took a vote, and it was a yes. I thought it would be great exposure for the band, and it was. Over the years, still to this day, people say, "The way I found out about you guys was through that Ace Ventura movie." It was exciting, and was definitely the right choice.

Cannibal Corpse went down to Miami and hung out on set with Jim Carrey and Courtney Cox while they filmed their parts. Chris Barnes ended up hanging around with Courtney a lot. They talked every day—to the extent that Chris thought she might have actually been flirting with him. He had a girlfriend at the time, so he didn't pursue it. Then, a few weeks later, she started dating the guy from Counting Crows, who looks very similar to Chris Barnes! I always say to Chris, "Dude, if only you hadn't had a girlfriend, we could've been hanging out on the set of *Friends*!"

Chris Barnes

We were hanging out before the shoot one day while Jim Carrey was getting his makeup and wardrobe done in the trailer. He was sitting with his little boom box playing Napalm Death, Pantera, AC/DC—all that kind of stuff.

Prior to the movie coming out in general release, I got an invitation to a private screening in LA with the producers and director. "What am I going to do if this movie sucks?" I remember thinking as I walked in. When I saw it, all those fears evaporated. It was so brilliant, and has become legendary—which is a huge credit to Jim Carrey, who somehow worked wonders on what I thought was a really dull script.

As it turned out, *Ace Ventura*, with that great scene where Jim Carrey joins the band onstage while they play "Hammer Smashed Face," was a huge benchmark in Cannibal Corpse's career. Something we never thought in a million years would amount to very much was responsible for taking Cannibal Corpse to an entirely new level. On paper, it was the most unlikely of partnerships, but the lesson it taught me is that, when presented with something off the wall, it's usually worth going into it with a "let's see what happens" attitude.

Contributing music to movies wasn't a totally new concept for Metal Blade. Back around 1985, in the days when we were working with Capitol, we were asked to provide an entire score, for lack of a better word, for a movie called *River's Edge*. It was a very dark movie about a high school kid (played by Keanu Reeves) who kills a girl. The producers specifically wanted heavy music throughout. The studio gave me the raw footage, maybe two hours in length at that early stage, and said, "Go through this and fit the music in." My first thought was how weird it was to watch a movie with absolutely no background music. I went through the whole thing, spent a week or so assembling it (Slayer, Fates Warning, and Hallows Eve were represented with tracks), and then gave it to back to them. They loved it. I was given a credit for my work. The story was based on true events and was pretty intense for that era. Many of the actors, most of whom were complete unknowns at the time, went on to have great careers. And the movie has since become a huge cult classic. It's fun to get into that game here and there, but as weird as the music business is, the movie world is a *lot* weirder!

Chapter 9
INDEPENDENCE RESTORED

We officially left Warner Bros. in late 1993 after Body Count left. It suited me to be independent once again, because it felt like that was how Metal Blade was always meant to be. While the volume of releases definitely slowed down somewhat, the mid-nineties brought opportunities to push the label forward, as the heavy music industry was still in a state of transition.

Being free of the limitations a corporate major label association involves allowed us to try some new things. We had been licensing music via Roadrunner for years, and it was hard to deny that Europe—Germany specifically (where we'd had a reciprocal licensing deal with Noise for many years)—was a significant market for heavy metal music.

It finally got to the point where we had such a big catalogue that it didn't make any sense *not* to have our own European office. We'd just lose money on our catalogue by having a third party selling for us. That would mean giving away 25 percent of a significant chunk of money, so we worked out that it would actually be cheaper to open an office there. Fortunately, Epitaph Records was in the process of doing the same thing, so the company that helped them relocate helped us, too.

While Germany was undeniably the strongest market, it certainly wasn't easy, from a tax and legal perspective, to just show up in a foreign country. Our first overseas office was actually in Holland, which everybody told us was the most US-friendly of the European countries when it came to setting up a remote office. It worked well, initially, principally because we hired a guy named

Michael Trengert, who had just left Nuclear Blast to start his own promotion company. He handled marketing and promotion for us, with his efforts primarily focused in Germany.

After a couple of years, we said to Michael, "You're doing such a great job, you should probably run this thing!" He said, "I'll run it, but you've got to move to Germany." So we made the move, and that's where we've been ever since. It was good to be in Europe, and we've signed tons of European bands since that office opened.

Although it wasn't directly related to our European presence, the signing of King Diamond and his band Mercyful Fate was one of the more exciting things that happened during the nineties. I'd been a massive fan since hearing that amazing demo while on my first trip to England with John Kornarens in 1982. I'd contacted them about being on *Metal Massacre* at the time, and it was scheduled to happen. Then, at the last minute, they ended up signing a deal with a small Dutch company, Rave-On Records, which put out the *Nuns Have No Fun* EP in 1982.

I continued to have a relationship with the guys in the band and their manager over the following years. I got to know King Diamond and became friendly with him. When he started having issues with Roadrunner as a solo artist in 1993, I said, "Well hey, I'll put my hand up here! Why don't you come to Metal Blade?"

I was also really hell-bent on working with his then-dormant band, Mercyful Fate, for a number of reasons. On one hand, I was a massive fan, and on the other, I always felt they had left the scene way too early. As it turned out, my passionate persistence was one of the factors that got Mercyful Fate back together.

Starting with *In the Shadows* and ending with *9*, Mercyful Fate released five albums with us from 1993 through 1999. To play a part in the process of putting a seminal band back together was another of the proudest achievements of my career. Unfortunately for them, the mid-nineties was arguably the *worst* time for an important metal band to get back together. I always thought their nineties output, though it was brilliant, got lost a little—certainly when compared with their seminal eighties records *Melissa* and *Don't Break the Oath.*

Nevertheless, all the records Mercyful Fate did with Metal Blade performed really well. They did a lot of great touring in the United States and played a ton of festivals in Europe. Sometimes it seems as if nobody knows about it now because that was the mid to late nineties, when metal was supposedly dead. Though it brought a lot of nostalgic warmth for me personally, their rebirth certainly didn't get the mainstream success I always felt the band's music deserved. Looking back, I think a lot people were just very happy that the band was back together at all.

The same applies to King Diamond, whose solo albums we released around the same time, starting with *The Spider's Lullabye* in 1995. People always talk about his early records—particularly *Fatal Portrait* and *Abigail*—but again, while I'm probably a little biased, there was some great stuff going on with his mid-nineties records.

Unfortunately, that whole era was just lost time. The metal mainstream went away during that period, but maybe it needed to. There were too many horrible groups calling themselves metal that weren't. I looked around at the worst of the hair bands and thought, "This isn't *my* heavy metal. This is just garbage." And I include the nu-metal movement in that characterization—with the caveat that Korn, which technically fell into that category, was undeniably interesting and momentarily crossed our radar.

Korn was from Bakersfield, California, and, at some point, Mike Faley had gone to a conference in San Diego where he caught one of their shows. He called me afterward. "Hey, I saw this band last night," he told me. "They were *incredible*. You've got to see them."

A couple of weeks later, we checked them out in LA at a club called The Dragonfly. There were only a couple hundred people there, but they were, as Faley had said, *incredible*—super heavy but also infused with something fresh and different. We started talking to them at the same time Roadrunner did. We were both tripping over ourselves to sign them. The next thing we knew, every major label on the planet was trying to get them. That was it; we had our moment, and we missed it. It became a crazy major label bidding war that we couldn't have competed with anyway.

But they were great. Both Korn and Tool got stuck into that nu-metal category, but neither of them, in my mind, really belonged in that world. All the other nonsense that came after them was, in my opinion, mostly horrible. Metal Blade just didn't touch it. Most of those bands felt to me like everything metal *wasn't*. I was always conscious of wanting to stay true to the metal genre and help it through those leaner years without compromising our values.

When people look back on that era, the only real metal band they ever talk about now is Pantera. It's become the lost decade for a lot of people, and that was tough on the bands that were putting out good music. I even remember *Rock Hard*—one of the major metal magazines in Europe—publishing an issue around 1997 that had a tombstone on the cover with the words *Heavy Metal: Born 1969, Died 1997*. Everybody, including the metal press, was writing the whole thing off, but I never felt that way.

There was no doubt that heavy metal needed to go back underground to reinvent itself, and that's what it gradually did. Still, when I look at some of the releases that came out on Metal Blade in the five-year period from 1995 to 2000, there was a lot to be optimistic about, particularly in the underground. Cannibal Corpse, Gwar, Mercyful Fate, and Six Feet Under (whose debut, *Haunted*, came out on Metal Blade in 1995) were all selling a lot of records. Interestingly, the evolution of Six Feet Under—a band that included Chris Barnes of Cannibal Corpse and Allen West of Obituary—happened almost by accident.

Chris was hanging out a lot with Allen West when Cannibal Corpse was getting pretty big, leading up to the release of *The Bleeding* in 1994. They were jamming on a lot of different musical styles that were slower than a lot of the fast death metal stuff that was prevalent at the time. Chris was a huge fan of traditional eighties metal bands like Priest and Maiden and, when they were just goofing around, Allen gave him a couple of really slow, simple riffs to sing over. Chris, who really dug what they were coming up with, said to me, "You know, I think I'd really like to do an EP or something outside of Cannibal."

"That's awesome," I responded. "Why not?" That eventually led to Chris and Allen doing an album. We really just put it out as a side project for them both, but, all of a sudden, Chris left Cannibal Corpse, and Six Feet Under became his full-time gig.

Chris Barnes

It was almost an accident. I wasn't happy where I was at. I was starting to think about other things. I was on tour with Obituary and got to talking to Trevor Peres about maybe doing a side project. He was one of the people I wanted to talk to about it. Then, when we were in Albuquerque, I got an introduction to Allen West in the back of the Obituary bus. We sat down and talked, hit it off, and it turned out that Allen wanted to do something, too. He said, "I already have five or six songs." So it went from there. The day I finished writing lyrics for The Bleeding *was the same day I started writing lyrics for* Haunted. *I had already talked to Brian about it and sent him some of the material. He thought it was an interesting idea.*

I should say I didn't agree with Cannibal Corpse when they let Chris go. I thought it was a terrible idea on the surface. Just when they were getting to be a massive band, they kicked out their lead singer! It made no sense. I remember saying to Alex Webster, "You don't *really* want to do that, do you? Are you guys crazy?"

Chris Barnes

As Cannibal Corpse's lineup changed, I started feeling uneasy. When Bob Rusay was forced out of the band, I felt like there was a change in the vibe. There was a balance there before, and when Bob went, that was lost. Everything went to one side and, at that point, I felt like I was set off in the corner. I saw Six Feet Under as my way out, and I worked hard at it. I was lucky enough that Brian supported me through that. He was told by the guys in Cannibal Corpse that they wanted to change vocalists, and I don't think he was too happy about it.

Although I heard both sides of the story, I wasn't really privy to
the precise details as to why Chris left Cannibal Corpse. I believe
it was just one of those age-old things where musical differences
came to the fore. Some people end up wanting to go in directions
that are incompatible with the confines of a particular band.
These things happen. But they split and, thankfully, it worked
out well for both parties. In fact, Six Feet Under's second record,
1997's *Warpath*, was bigger than any Cannibal Corpse record at
that time—and Cannibal would obviously go on to have a hugely
successful career in their own right.

※

In addition to the death metal stuff, more established bands like
Fates Warning, Flotsam and Jetsam, and Sacred Reich were all
putting out strong releases that did well commercially. Anvil was on
the label at that time, too (*Anthology of Anvil*, 1999).

I often think we were able to survive the whole tough decade of
the nineties specifically by *not* turning our back on the metal scene
and culture. Not everyone did the same. A lot of others declared
it dead and got out altogether. Still others, perhaps too influenced
by the grunge scene, started signing bands that were patently non-
metal. We didn't do that; we just kept signing the kind of bands
that we signed, while staying engaged in the broader environment
via marketing and promotion.

As well as the success of Goo Goo Dolls, which definitely didn't
hurt, our third party marketing and promotional activities were
pretty key in terms of navigating what I thought were worrisome,
but definitely non-terminal times. In some ways, we had the best of
both worlds. Grunge was there, and there was nothing we could do
about it. But we had the marketing and promotional angle, a big
catalogue that was still selling, reissues of material that had yet to
see the light of day on CD, and, of course, our own underground
acts filling in the holes wherever possible. We found a way to make
things work. All you can do in the face of change is adapt.

An Interview with King Diamond

How did your relationship with Metal Blade begin?

I was moving my whole operation from Denmark to Dallas in 1992. You could say it was a business decision. We had ended our deal with Roadrunner and we were talking to Warner Denmark. I wouldn't quite say they misled us, but we didn't know exactly what they were about. We had conversations, and then they said, "When we release the next album, if it goes well in Scandinavia, we can look into releasing it in Germany." I said, "Wait a minute here. Are you telling us we're not going to have a worldwide release?"

They didn't know what we'd done in the past. I said, "Forget it." I needed to go where the business was, and, at that time, it was the US.

Our lawyer in New York told me that, while he was shopping us in the US, Brian and Metal Blade were interested in doing business with us with a view to discussing both bands. At that time, it was a little complicated because King Diamond was running full power, but Mercyful Fate was not. That said, when I arrived in the US, I had some musical ideas that felt like they would be suited to Mercyful Fate. I didn't want to waste them, so the idea had occurred to me. And then, when Brian signed us, with both of us having a separate contract, he decided that he wanted to do a Mercyful Fate record first. It was a perfect collision of purposes: I had music, and Brian was desperate to put out a Mercyful Fate album.

Were you aware how big a fan Brian was?

Brian knew every little detail about us. I didn't know that he'd got the first EP, but then he told me that he and Lars Ulrich had sat in Lars's apartment when they got a physical copy of it, and they both freaked out. He was way into us long before we became connected, and, since those early days, Brian and I have become very close. Any decisions we make are made together, both of us sitting in a room or a restaurant, with no lawyers. We're just two guys working out the best thing for us both. That's how it's always been.

Have there been difficult times, too?

Definitely—particularly around the time of Abigail II *in 2002. That was about the time when downloading had really started picking up. It was hard for a label like Metal Blade to continue giving tour support to bands, which was a tough time for all of us. There was never huge money offered to get a tour started, but it was always important money. We didn't tour much for one album, and that impacts everything—particularly when you find out later that your music is being shared for free online.*

I had a good friend who used to work for the police in San Antonio, and he did a bit of checking for us one day. What he told me was really demoralizing. He let me know how many people were in line to download our albums—and these could have been sales otherwise. We're talking 80,000. It was completely out of control. And you can only sit there, unable to do anything. Nobody can shut it down. When illegal things are allowed to happen that affect your livelihood, it's very tough. But you have to try and find ways to get around it.

And you and Metal Blade survived.

Brian and Metal Blade remind me a lot of how my relationship was with Roadrunner in the early days. Metal Blade survives through hardships, and I think that has a lot to do with the fact that they're always on top of whatever is new. I like the way that, when they sign new bands, it's not always just one person who makes the decision. The entire staff gets to hear the music for a little while, and then they come back with opinions. While they may not have the final decision, they are always consulted.

I guess it goes back to the fundamental fact that Brian was and is a fan of this music?

He is still that major fan. He is. He was here one night at my house, listening to some music. I had just gotten these new handmade speakers that sounded insanely good. They don't lie. So I said to him, "What's your favorite song? Let me play it for you." It was an Iron Maiden song—I can't remember which one—and during the drum intro, these speakers revealed a reverb that Brian had never heard before. He couldn't believe it. He said, "What? What version is this?" I said, "No, this is the original CD from when it came out." It was so interesting for me to observe how much it meant to him to hear something that he had never heard in that way before. That's Brian Slagel's passion right there.

Sounds like you have a lot in common?

Yes, we do. We listen to things in similar ways. I remember once when we were talking about the band City Boy and the album Young Men Gone West. *I had loved that band from back in the seventies, and it turned out he did, too. We like a lot of the same styles, and it's easy to hit it off with someone like that. I also really value Brian's upfront way of dealing with things—that was the same with Cees Wessels at Roadrunner. They both have allowed me to ask questions, and I really value Brian's expertise.*

How much input does Brian have creatively?

I usually run any new ideas for new ventures by him first. We have completely open doors; we sit at a round table and talk. It's in nobody's interest to fight, so every issue is discussed. For example, we're working on a Blu-ray disc of an indoor and an outdoor show from recent festivals. To have more than one show, however, was not part of the original agreement we had. I presented it to Brian and said, "I know it's not in the deal, but…" He could have said, "No, it's not a good idea." But he didn't. Sometimes when he does show some hesitancy, my artistic side kicks in. There are certain things, from a creative standpoint, that I feel compelled to do. I can't compromise who I am, and I can't lie, either. But we always end up with a solution, so there will be an indoor and outdoor show on the disc!

How would you sum up Brian Slagel and Metal Blade?

I have the highest respect for Brian. I consider him a very close friend. And because we don't have management—we are our own management—I get to work with a lot of the other support staff at Metal Blade, too. We all work amazingly well together.

With the new millennium upon us, the way people were experiencing music was gradually changing. From that perspective, it made no sense to continue with the *Metal Massacre* compilation series beyond 1996.

The reason we'd started it in the first place was to give a platform to bands that otherwise might never get heard. In those days, long before YouTube, there were no other ways for people to access new music. And, for many years, the series was successful in fulfilling the needs of both the artists and the audience. At a certain point in time, however, there were just so many record labels out there that pretty much every band was getting signed quickly and easily. There was no need to continue with *Metal Massacre*.

We had plenty of other artists and releases to focus on, and some new ones were appearing on our radar, too. I'd been a huge fan of King's X since they broke out in 1988. *Out of the Silent Planet* is still one of my favorite records of all time. I eventually became really good friends with the band, and it always bothered me that they, like many others, never became as big as they really should have.

I've always had my theories as to why that might have been, but I think a big part of it was that their debut was so amazing and groundbreaking that they got caught between a bunch of scenes without really fitting neatly into any one of them. They were also an unusual band from an aesthetic standpoint. You don't see a lot of three-piece groups where the lead singer is a really tall, thin, black bassist with a Mohawk. Nobody knew where to place them—especially mainstream radio.

When King's X reached the end of the road on Atlantic in 1997, we approached them. They signed with us, and we released *Tapehead* in 1998, followed by five more albums up until 2005.

※

When the new millennium arrived, I viewed it as yet another turning point in heavy music. The early 1980s were huge. Then, in the early 1990s, metal receded and was replaced by grunge. There was an obvious ebb and flow at play, and, from my perspective, another flow occurred around 2000.

It felt like we'd moved beyond the whole "metal is dead" way of thinking and, shortly afterward, there was a resurgence of heavy music that has carried the genre right through to the present day.

As an example, a couple of guys who worked for Metal Blade—Dan Fitzgerald and E. J. Johantgen—came and told me they wanted to start a label of their own just before the start of the new millennium. I had no problem with it whatsoever, and we even ended up collaborating on a few things with their label, which they called Prosthetic Records.

To get them started, we put Prosthetic through our distribution channel and helped with promotion to the point where we were almost treating their releases as we would Metal Blade projects. Because they had no money and couldn't compensate us financially, they offered to give us a small share in the label. I agreed, and we proceeded on those terms. From my perspective, there wasn't much to lose. They were doing some good things with some really cool bands, and while I didn't know where it would all ultimately end, I was fine with getting them started. They're still in existence today, albeit no longer distributed by Metal Blade (although Dan is still a Metal Blade employee). They still ask me questions now and again, and I'll always help them out whenever I can.

One of the bands that was on Prosthetic's radar at the beginning was Burn the Priest from Richmond, Virginia. Prosthetic knew about them before most people and, recognizing the potential, were aggressively pursuing them. They came to us wondering whether we'd consider some sort of joint venture.

Because I was happy to mentor these colleagues, the first thing I said was, "Look, if you want this band to be really big—and they look like they could be—you need to get them to change that name." As much as I was a fan of pushing the envelope, freaking people out, and getting as close to the edge as humanly possible,

I knew that a band going by the name Burn the Priest was never going to be anything other than an underground act.

I fully expected the band to say, "Fuck you," but they didn't. They understood the rationale and agreed to change the name to Lamb of God. Then they went out with Gwar on their first national tour in support of their debut, *New American Gospel*. We got them started, and they went on to become huge.

When you heard bands like Lamb of God, Unearth, and As I Lay Dying—two of which we signed—you could tell there was a groundswell of something new on the way. There was a mix of metal and hardcore at play, and the reason it all worked, sparking a major resurgence in the 2000s, was that you had bands that were influenced on a sociological level by hardcore, but at the same time were shaped by a lot of the early metal stuff.

Hardcore brought with it a "We're in this together" mentality of brotherhood, while metal had the music to fuse with that spirit. The rumblings started in 2000 and just kept going. It really felt like some good days might be ahead.

When we signed acts like As I Lay Dying (2003), The Black Dahlia Murder (2003), and Unearth (2004), I was as excited about metal as I'd ever been in the past. Everywhere you looked, there were these fresh bands, and when you talked to these kids, they were so humble and cool. I had noticed that, up until the early 2000s, nobody had ever really given any respect to the *history* of heavy metal. With the exception of Metallica, who had always talked a lot about who came before them, artists never really mentioned their influences in interviews. It just wasn't a big thing to acknowledge history.

Suddenly you had these twenty-year-old kids appearing on the scene who had an astute awareness of, and appreciation for, the lineage that preceded them—all the way back to the early 1980s. I remember having a conversation with Phil Sgrosso, the guitar player in As I Lay Dying. He was starting to really get into music from the seventies and eighties like UFO and Thin Lizzy. "Hey man," he said to me one day, "can you make me a CD with your top Thin Lizzy songs on it?" Then another time he called me and said, "I heard *Rainbow Rising* is really good. Should I buy it?" I said, "You should drop the phone immediately and go get it."

In creating a new scene, these bands were also reigniting the old one and repurposing it for a new era. All of a sudden, these guys were wearing the old t-shirts and talking in interviews about how much they loved Iron Maiden and Rainbow.

As someone who'd been in it from the very beginning, it was so gratifying to see things coming full circle. Not just that—I was every bit as excited to be involved in the future of the genre as I was to have a stake in the past. Because these new bands' fans were also young kids in their early twenties, when they saw their idols wearing Priest t-shirts and talking about Maiden, it was completely logical that they latched onto that and went out and discovered all those bands for themselves, too.

While I'm never a fan of any of the convenient terms for styles of music within a broad genre, there's no doubt that the term "metalcore" *did* accurately describe what these newer bands were doing. I was OK with it, and there could have been many worse names attached to it all. Of all the bands that we signed at that time, the one that was most representative of the whole scene was As I Lay Dying. They became, by far, the biggest of any of those similar acts. Having said that, the band that got the whole ball rolling in earnest was Unearth.

We signed Unearth in 2003, after they had basically agreed to sign with another label. Everyone, including me, had loved their debut release, *The Stings of Conscience*, which came out two years prior. They were due to play a show in LA before we signed them, so I contacted their management to arrange to meet the guys. The manager was lukewarm. "Yeah, you can go," I was told, "but they're pretty much committed to signing with someone else."

We went in really softly and never discussed anything business-related. A couple of days later, we got a call from their manager saying, "I don't know what you guys did or said, but the band now wants to trash this other deal and sign with you!"

For whatever reason, they liked the vibe we had going on. When we put out *The Oncoming Storm* in 2004, it exploded, and they sang our praises. That had a domino effect, in terms of attracting other bands. We could have signed pretty much any group from that scene that we wanted to. There was real credibility established that really helped, since we were not initially frontrunners in the metalcore movement.

The Oncoming Storm was one of those records where the timing was absolutely right and, as a result, it far exceeded any of our expectations. I knew the scene was happening, and that there was a lot of cool stuff going on, but the reaction to *The Oncoming Storm* was on a different level than everything else.

Another band that came along at that time was Amon Amarth. I'll never forget being over in the European office in Germany when one of the guys there said, "I've heard this new band Amon Amarth, and you might want to sign them." I checked them out, thought they were great, and said, "Let's do it."

They had started out as a death metal band in the European melodic style, but then, in 2004, they released *Fate of Norms*, and that, like Unearth's debut, became a touchstone for our activity in that decade. Up until that point, they'd been a proficient melodic death metal band, but, all of a sudden, they'd taken this turn that changed everything. I remember hearing the early demos and saying. "This is *really* interesting. You guys are taking a huge step up with this stuff." The music, the songwriting, and the structures were all much improved.

With that said, when I got the first mix, I wasn't impressed. "The music is really good," I told them, "but the mix needs work. We have to do something about this." They were always really easy to work with, so we fixed the mix and were able to create a really amazing record. Now they're one of the biggest bands on Metal Blade—and in all of heavy metal.

Fate of Norms further reinforced the sense that interesting things were happening. Amon Amarth didn't fit into the metalcore category in any way; they definitely had their own thing going on, and they continued that trajectory of evolving closer to the mainstream while still retaining much of their original fan base. *Fate of Norms* was probably the record that most tested the fans' loyalty. While it ended up doing very well, a few of the diehards who had latched onto the very early stuff were saying they weren't into it. Initially, it was a little rough, but, like any band, the key is to gain more than you lose. And Amon Amarth *definitely* did that.

Equally significant to the label—and heavy music in general— was Whitechapel. They'd released one record, *The Somatic Defilement*, in 2006. Soon after, a lawyer named Bryan Christner, who has represented a bunch of bands on Metal Blade, came to us. "I'm looking for a deal for this band from Knoxville, Tennessee," he explained. "Are you interested?" We said, "Sure, send us the record, and we'll have a listen." They sent us the debut album, which was very good, and we started talking to one of their guitar players, Alex Wade, who was the main guy in the band.

Two things struck me about them right off the bat: One, they were incredibly young. Two, they were from *Knoxville*, which seemed as far removed from any scene as you could possibly get, yet these young guys totally had it together, and we knew they could become successful all around the world. Knoxville might seem like a random place, but it just goes to show how the music has become a worldwide phenomenon. You never know where people are listening to metal as they're growing up.

We signed Whitechapel, released *This Is Exile* in 2008, and, with some exposure on the Mayhem Festival tour and a lot of hard work, they've become one of the flagship acts on Metal Blade.

More great bands kept coming our way. Based on a connection with Paul Conroy, who was Unearth's manager in the early 2000s, Behemoth soon appeared on the Metal Blade radar. I was a huge fan and loved the band, so I told Paul and his Good Fight Management team that we were absolutely interested in signing them.

Initially it was going to be a worldwide deal, but Michael Trengert, who was running our European office, wasn't feeling it at all. It was the only time we ever had a battle over whether to sign a band. As a compromise, we agreed to do a deal exclusively for North America at first. We released *Evangelion* in 2009, and we loved working with the band and their lead singer, Nergal. As the catalogue became available, we went back and reissued pretty much all of it on Metal Blade.

After the great success of *Evangelion,* Nergal was diagnosed with leukemia. It was a particularly scary situation for me, given what had happened to Armored Saint's Dave Prichard. I was freaking out initially, but, after doing some research, it became obvious that leukemia wasn't necessarily the death sentence it had once been. Fortunately, Nergal pulled through, but it was scary for a while.

That same year, 2009, was significant in that Behemoth—and four other Metal Blade bands—entirely took over the Hot Topic stage at that year's Mayhem Festival. It should have been called the Metal Blade stage!

European metal festivals have been a big help throughout the last thirty-five years. In the mid to late 2000s, the Ozzfest and Mayhem Festivals really boosted the scene, specifically thanks to the concept of the second stage. We started putting bands on those second stages and saw a tangible benefit. All of a sudden, instead of a group playing in front of a thousand people, they were playing in front of five thousand. Consequently, all the bands that ended up on these stages did extremely well.

For example, as big as Cannibal Corpse was by 2009, that year's Mayhem Festival—where they played last on the second stage— really boosted their popularity even further. People knew who they were, but had never actually seen them live. That tour elevated them to a completely new level of popularity. It was insane seeing the fans go completely crazy.

An Interview with Johan Hegg of Amon Amarth

Is your interest in Norse history/mythology an inherent part of your upbringing? Has the subject always interested you?

It wasn't part of my upbringing, but of course I knew about Vikings from an early age. It wasn't until I was around ten years old that I started to develop a real interest in the history and mythology of my ancestors. It began with reading about it in literature class, and then I read the Valhalla comic book series by Peter Madsen. I was completely hooked. From there I started reading the actual Viking sagas and legends, such as Njal's Saga *and* Egil Skallagrimson's *Saga, and of course the* Poetic Edda, *which is the mythology in poetic form.*

What were the circumstances surrounding the band signing to Metal Blade? Can you give me a sense of the scene in Sweden prior to that?

Well, we had released our mini-CD, Sorrow Throughout the Nine Worlds, *on a small, newly started label from Singapore called Pulverized Records. The release caught the interest of several labels that then got in touch with us. Nuclear Blast was the first big one, but we were hesitant about signing with them, since they already had so many bands on their roster that were similar to us. Still, it was the best deal we had received, so we were considering signing with them. Then a contract proposal came in the mail from Metal Blade. The offer was just so much better than what Nuclear Blast had put forth, so, after consulting an attorney, we decided to sign with Metal Blade, and I believe it was the perfect choice for us. We've had a great relationship with Metal Blade throughout our career. That's why we've stayed with them for so long.*

Were you ever aware of the concept of "Viking metal"? And by that, I mean was there ever a conscious decision to carve out a specific space for the band to occupy?

The first time I ever heard the term "Viking metal" was actually in the early nineties in relation to the band Enslaved, from Norway. We called ourselves "melodic Viking death metal" in the beginning—mainly to distance ourselves lyrically from other melodic death metal bands. It wasn't our intention to make the Viking theme our concept at first, but, as things progressed, it became natural to keep writing about those topics. It was something we all felt strongly about and that we felt worked well with the music we were creating.

How much input does Metal Blade have, in terms of your music, if any? Brian mentioned that he questioned how a record was mixed. Can you remember?

Metal Blade has never interfered with our writing process. Brian said once that he wanted to come visit us in the studio during the recording—I think that was during the making of Deceiver of the Gods*—but we told him he wasn't welcome in the studio before the album was recorded! Of course, Brian has had thoughts about the mixes that we've presented at times, but that is only natural. In general, it's been very easy to work with him.*

There was a significant turning point, it seems, with the release of *Jornsviking*. Was there a conscious effort to align yourselves more with the mainstream than previously, or was this just natural progression?

Not really. I honestly feel we haven't changed that much. I guess it's because we've never been afraid to reach out to different crowds without changing what we do. I think if you do try to change who you are and what you do just to reach a mainstream audience, you're treading some really dangerous waters. If you're honest with yourself and true to who you are, people will appreciate it more.

Many people have described being a Metal Blade artist as being part of a family. Can you resonate with that?

Absolutely! It is a very familial atmosphere, and I've felt that way since day one. For instance, I remember calling Brian Slagel up after the original recording of our debut, Once Sent from the Golden Hall, *got fucked up in the recording at Sunlight Studios in Stockholm. I had not even met Brian back then. I hadn't even talked to him over the phone, but I was in a position where I pretty much had to call him and tell him that we needed to re-record the album in the Abyss Studios with Peter Tägtgren. I was very nervous, to say the least, but Brian was calm and just said, "Well, you still have budget left, and I will talk to Studio Sunlight to get them to cut the costs, since we can't use what they produced for us." We went to the Abyss Studios, and the result came out great, considering all the turmoil.*

Chapter 10
EMBRACING
THE UNEXPECTED

The debut albums from As I Lay Dying and The Black Dahlia Murder were two releases that were of great significance to us during the 2000s. The Black Dahlia Murder was one of the weirdest signings in the history of the label. Late one night I was trolling Myspace, which was where everybody went at that time to listen to music. I noticed, when looking at a few of the pages of bands I knew, that several of them were connected to The Black Dahlia Murder. I clicked on their page, where they had two or three songs. They were incredible!

I reached out through Myspace. "Hey, I'm from Metal Blade," I wrote, "and your stuff sounds really good. What are you guys doing?" As it turned out, they were just about to sign a deal with another label, though not a big one. When they found out we were interested, their thinking changed. I'd never signed a band by randomly looking around the internet, but they just appeared, and everything came together.

The Black Dahlia Murder was already a great band, but when it came to making that first record, *Unhallowed*, they really stepped up and made a phenomenal musical statement that reflected so many influences. It was a perfectly balanced mix of super melodic metal with really crazy vocals. I still love that record. With most albums, you're kind of over it once you've listened to the demos and the masters many times over in the production process. But even when the CD came out, I just couldn't stop listening to it.

When I look back on the whole early to mid-2000s period, it surprises me to see how all-over-the-map we were in terms of the styles of the bands we had on the label. We had the underground bands that had been the mainstay through the nineties, and we had the classic bands that had been there since the beginning. Then we had this whole new raft of metalcore acts, and also new material from melodic metal bands like Masquerade (*Flux*, 2001), Labyrinth (*Sons of Thunder*, 2000), and Memory Garden (*Mirage*, 2000). On top of that, we were re-releasing a lot of old school New Wave of British Heavy Metal material, such as Holocaust, Savage, Quartz, and Jaguar. The roster was all over the place, and it was pretty interesting to be a part of it. As diverse as the list was, all of it did really well.

Given that genuine heavy metal was on the way back in, it was entirely appropriate that we should get the opportunity to work with Manowar—a band that not only epitomized the heavy metal attitude, but one that I'd always loved since my very early days with the fanzine.

We got the opportunity to work with them because they didn't have a label and I, as I did with most bands in that limbo situation, started talking to them. The coolest part of it is that the record we did with them, *Warriors of the World*, pretty much brought them back to where they'd been in the eighties—certainly in terms of a US audience. The nineties hadn't been kind to them in the States, but in Europe it was always a different story; they regularly played arenas.

Consequently, I pretty much *made* them tour *Warriors of the World* in the United States. They went out with Six Feet Under and did really well. It was one of the only full US tours that Manowar ever did, and it really pumped up sales of the album. We did some further studio records and some live material with them, which further strengthened their position. Not everybody is going to say that Manowar is easy to work with, but, from my perspective, they couldn't have been more of a pleasure.

�֎

One of the many joys of being in this business is discovering all the other people around my age—who work in all kinds of other industries, sometimes in some very major roles—who are diehard metal fans like I am. Almost without fail, when I'm in a room or a restaurant—or really anywhere—I'll find someone in their forties or fifties who has been into heavy metal forever. That has prompted me to attempt to attract more fans to metal by pairing the music with other activities, such as sports, comedy, or other forms of spoken media.

The first such example of two seemingly separate worlds merging actually took place back in the eighties, thanks to my obsession with ice hockey. As I mentioned, I had a contact who got me tickets to LA Kings games. Over time, I got to know some inside people who worked in the hockey world. As fascinated as I was with their experiences, they were equally intrigued by my career in the music business.

During the late eighties, the Kings had a player named Ken Baumgartner. He was a super intimidating enforcer guy. He'd originally been playing at the Kings' farm team—the New Haven Nighthawks in Connecticut—and, as it turned out, the original bass player from Fates Warning (Joe DeBiase, who also lived in New Haven) was a season ticket holder. He called me one day. "The Kings have just signed this guy Ken Baumgartner," he told me. "You're going to love him."

Ken quickly became pretty famous in the LA community as an uncompromising player. He was a huge fan favorite, and his nickname was "Bomber." In 1989, one of my friends who worked at *Hockey News*—which was the be-all and end-all of hockey information in those days—came up with the concept of approaching Ken with the idea of collaborating on a single. The obvious song choice was "Bomber" by Motörhead. I had no idea whether he'd be into it in any way, but, to my surprise, when they presented it to him, he said, "Yeah, that would be great, as long as the proceeds go to a charity."

I was excited by the idea and immediately started assembling a little all-star band featuring Mark Zonder from Fates Warning on drums, Joey Vera of Armored Saint and Fates Warning on bass, Rocky George from Suicidal Tendencies on guitar, and Armored Saint's John Bush to help him sing. Everyone went into the studio together to record "Bomber" and a couple of other songs. While Ken couldn't sing at all, he worked very hard and was a great sport. The Kings were aware we were doing it, so they came and filmed the recording session to show in between periods at a later game.

We sent the recording to Jim Rome, the sports talk show host, since we knew a few of the people who worked on his show were super into metal. He started getting Ken to call in, and he was a riot. Underneath the tough-guy image that Ken Baumgartner perpetuated on the ice, he was an extremely smart guy who would go on to get an MBA from Harvard after he quit hockey.

Over the years, I've become good friends with athletes who are big metal fans, as well as people who work within major sports franchises who also love the genre. One of my buddies, Shawn Roarke, who runs NHL.com, came to me in 2010 and suggested we create a "sports and metal" podcast. We did a couple episodes for fun by getting some NHL guys to come in and talk. It worked well, so we officially launched *Metal Misconduct* in 2011. We've been doing it ever since. We've had NHL players, NFL players, MMA fighters—you name it, we've had them on.

It's great fun to hear these sports guys talking about something other than their job. Those kinds of interviews tend to be dull and cliché, anyway. While there probably aren't as many metalhead sports stars out there as there used to be, I'm still pleasantly surprised when I find that pretty much every sport has a bunch of metal guys—hockey especially.

From baseball, we've had Hall of Famer Randy Johnson on the podcast. Mike Piazza, another Hall of Famer, has also been on. As a huge fan of Indy Car, it was no surprise to me that there are a bunch of guys who work in that business who are huge metalheads, too—including some of the drivers.

I've been amazed by who's out there listening to our bands. I suppose I sometimes get caught up in the bubble of what we do every day, and a part of me subconsciously thinks I'm still running a small thing from my mom's garage. It's not just sports guys who are fans, either—actors, comedians, people in other bands—and all kinds of other people from all walks of life who, despite huge success and fame, are really down-to-earth and just want to talk about music. The bottom line is that we do it all for fun, and to spread the word about metal.

※

Johan from Amon Amarth was hanging out at my house one day in 2013. "Hey, have you ever heard of this guy Chris Santos?" he asked.

"No," I replied. "Who is he?" Johan told me he was a celebrity chef judge from the TV show *Chopped,* which I'd never seen. As it turned out, Chris had some restaurants in New York and was a huge metalhead—to the extent that he came out on the Mayhem tour and cooked for everybody, including Amon Amarth. Johan said the food was incredible, and that the guy was a super cool dude.

I found Chris on Twitter and immediately started communicating with him. I later met him at a Slayer show, and we became friends through music. I'd never been to his restaurants, hadn't heard of the TV show, and didn't know anything about him. Yet (much like other people from different circles I've met on my travels over the years) we had a great connection through heavy metal—and he was a huge fan of Metal Blade.

After a while, I thought to myself, "I've known this guy for a while now. I should really go to one of his restaurants!" It was some of the best food I've ever had in my life.

Chris Santos

I'm a complete lifer. I'm basically obsessed with metal and have been since as long as I can remember. When I was eleven or twelve, this girl in my neighborhood played me Don't Break the Oath *by Mercyful Fate. That was it for me. By the time I was fourteen, I was sneaking off to see bands like Dark Angel and Possessed. I lived in a small town in Rhode Island, and I'd jump on the bus every Saturday to go to the record store to pick up whatever new vinyl was coming out. I knew who Brian was and what Metal Blade was in 1987; pretty much everything I was buying seemed to be on that label.*

Chris and I became very good friends, and he started turning me on to a bunch of bands. Because his life is so busy, his way of winding down is to scour the internet looking for new music. Gradually he started introducing me to bands I'd never heard of, like an incredible instrumental group called If These Trees Could Talk, which Metal Blade ended up signing. Then he turned me on to Mother Feather, which we also signed, as well as Canderia, whose members we persuaded to get back together and do a record with us. It got to the point where I eventually said to Chris, "Look, if you want to be an A&R guy for us, or want to have a label or something, we should do it." He said, "I don't want to take your money. I'm just doing this for fun!"

A couple of weeks after we signed another band called Harm's Way that Chris pointed out to me, I met up with him at a show in New York. "All right," he said. "That's it. I changed my mind. Give me a label!"

So now Chris is on board with his own imprint called Blacklight Media, and he has already signed a few really good bands—the first one being Good Tiger, which is a bit of a super-group of guys from Architects and Tesseract.

He's not on the payroll per se, but Blacklight is a satellite imprint from which Metal Blade gets paid on the back end. It has worked really well so far, mainly because Chris has very interesting taste in bands that differs from what we'd normally do on Metal Blade.

Chris Santos

My initial reservation about having an imprint was because I'm so busy with my work. I didn't think I'd have the time for it, but Brian and everyone at Metal Blade have made it so easy by doing all the heavy lifting. I just get to go out and scout bands and, if I like them, I say, "Hey Brian, listen to this. What do you think?" What's beautiful about Blacklight is that it gives Metal Blade another vehicle through which to sign bands that might not be traditionally Metal Blade–type bands.

Obviously, we've done a few label collaborations over the years, but it has been particularly interesting to do something with a guy like Chris, because he has a whole cache of mainstream publicity that we just couldn't access otherwise. He's on *Good Morning America* and in the *Wall Street Journal*—outlets that Metal Blade would never be seen in. I just tag along for the ride.

Chris Santos

I'm on a Food Network show and am a kind of celebrity of sorts in the food world, so when we broke news of the Blacklight label, it was launched on Wall Street Journal*—not a place where you'd normally expect news of a new metal label to be released. But, because of my status, we have an opportunity to reach outlets that we wouldn't have otherwise. The result is that I get a tremendous amount of demos sent my way. I don't have to search so hard now!*

Something similar happened with Monte Pittman. Monte moved from Dallas to LA in 1999 and started working at Guitar Center in Hollywood. Like people do when they're trying to make extra money in LA, he put up a card in the store advertising guitar lessons. One of the first people to take the card was someone associated with Brad Pitt. Before long, Monte was teaching Brad Pitt to play the guitar. From there, he taught Guy Oseary, Madonna's manager. Then he taught Jennifer Aniston and, eventually, he became Madonna's guitar teacher. It's crazy to think this kid from Texas was teaching all these famous people how to play guitar.

After he'd been teaching Madonna for just a few weeks, she said, "I'm doing *Letterman* next week and need an acoustic guitar player. Can you come and do it?" He went, played the show, and has now been Madonna's guitarist for almost fifteen years.

Monte had done some solo material and, in 2012, was working on a metal record with Flemming Rasmussen, the producer of the great Metallica albums *Ride the Lightning, Master of Puppets* and *...And Justice for All.* Around that same time, Chris Barnes had met Monte and introduced him to me. It turned out that he'd always been a huge fan of Metal Blade. Monte played me some of the material in his car that would later become his first Metal Blade record, *The Power of Three.* He wasn't looking for a deal at the time, so much as a bit of advice, but I thought it was really good and asked him to send me a copy. I took it to the office to get some other opinions on it. Everyone agreed that it was really strong. We signed him and have done two solo records, both of which are great. It was another cool project that came out of nowhere.

※

Comedy is another medium that has always been very important to me, dating all the way back to the early 1980s, before Metal Blade properly existed. Lizzy Borden and his brother used to hang out at The Comedy Store all the time. We were all big fans, but those two were in Hollywood pretty much every night. Somebody told them about a guy called Sam Kinison before anyone had ever heard of him. Lizzy came to me one day. "Dude, you've *got* to go see this guy," he told me. "He's hysterical."

One Tuesday night, we headed to The Comedy Store. There were maybe ten people in the audience, if that. We watched a bunch of acts, and then, at around 1:30 in the morning, Sam took the stage. I have never laughed so hard in my entire life. My cheeks hurt; my stomach hurt. The guy was unbelievable.

Soon, we started going all the time. Sam would do five nights a week, closing The Comedy Store when there was almost nobody there. As time passed, he must have thought, "Who are these metal guys who are always here?" Gradually, we started becoming friends with him. My girlfriend at the time was also really good friends with a girl Sam was dating, so we went out to dinner once or twice.

One night after a show, as we were hanging out having drinks, I said, "I've got this little record label. It's still very small and just doing metal stuff. But maybe we could do a comedy record if you wanted to do something?"

"That sounds really cool," he said, "but I've just gotten this offer to do an HBO show with Rodney Dangerfield." At the time, Rodney had an HBO special where he'd pick five or ten comedians and put them on for five minutes each. Sam wanted to see what would happen with that and, of course, he exploded and became a phenomenon.

Since then, I've always been a big fan of comedy, and always thought it would be fun to somehow merge that world with metal. We'd dabbled with it over the years—talking to guys like Brian Posehn—and then, finally, around 2012, I'd heard that the comedian Jim Florentine was a big metal fan. Somebody introduced me to him somewhere and we started talking, and it turned out he was a major Raven fan. I told him I had a bunch of old tapes, and our friendship developed from there.

At one point, we were sitting around, and I said, "Why don't you do a comedy record for us?" He loved the idea, so that's what we did in 2013. I met Don Jamieson soon after, so we signed a deal with him, too. In fact, Don's record came out before Jim's did, even though I met Jim first. Those guys are hilarious and went on to have success with *That Metal Show*.

It felt great to make something happen with comedy. We'd toyed with it for years, but the timing had never felt quite right. It's really fun to do, but it's a different world in terms of marketing. It's very difficult, but all we're looking for is some crossover, and to capitalize on the considerable cool factor attached with working with such great guys. Because these guys host a bunch of events for us, the tie-ins are really great. Overall, it's a cool look for Metal Blade.

Consequently, I got all kinds of comedians calling saying, "Let's do a record!" Eventually I had to say, "We're not a comedy label; we're a music label. I can't tell you that I totally know what I'm doing with comedy." But then Cory Brennan, who manages Slipknot and Amon Amarth, called me and said, "Hey, would you be interested in doing something with Jim Breuer?" My initial impulse, being a massive fan, was to say yes. I was invited down to see him, and we talked after the show. As it turned out, he wanted to do a real metal record, not a comedy record per se. Before I left, I said, "OK, this could be interesting. Let's keep talking about it." While we were on the freeway driving away after the show, Cory called me and said, "Jim has a song he'd like to play for you. How far away are you?"

"We're just an exit away," I said. "I can easily turn around." So, we went back, and Jim played us a song in his rented Toyota. It was actually really good. "I'm in," I said. We made a deal with Cory and then cut a record (with Rob Caggiano of Volbeat playing guitar and producing) that came out in 2016. We also had Brian Johnson of AC/DC sing on it, which was beyond insane. It's a real metal record, but with comedy overtones. That's exactly the kind of thing we can do as an independent label. A huge part of the appeal for me has always been to have the freedom to say "yes" to left-field ideas. If we were owned by somebody else, or had a partner, we probably wouldn't be able to have these kinds of adventures.

An Interview with comedian Don Jamieson

Where did your interest in metal music stem from? What were your early influences?

I got the Destroyer *album by Kiss when I was eleven years old, and I never turned back. That was my gateway record into hard rock and heavy metal. When you're eleven, a rock band whose members are also comic book characters and superheroes is about as cool as it gets.*

What led you into a comedy career?

Rampant truancy. No, honestly I always had a love for music and comedy since I was a kid. I played guitar in a band in high school, but, as I got older, I thought I might enjoy doing comedy more. You don't have to split the money with anyone, there's no drama, and no equipment to lug. I just put my dick jokes in my pocket and go.

Do you see comedy and metal as being pretty easy bedfellows, for want of a better expression?

Some of my comedy influences are actually musicians. Ozzy, to this day, still has amazing one-liners in interviews, like the Rodney Dangerfield of metal. The late Pete Steele was always self-deprecating, like the Steven Wright of goth, David Lee Roth was maniacally funny as hell, and out on his own planet, like a hard-rocking Robin Williams. And Alice Cooper always told amazing stories that would end with one great punch line, kind of like Bill Cosby without the bad sweaters and the 'ludes.

How did you first get to know Brian?

My comedy partner, Jim Florentine, had met him and hung out with him first, and then he told me that Brian had given him a bunch of Iron Maiden bootlegs. I was so jealous. I was a huge fan of the original Metal Massacre *albums and tons of the bands that appeared on Metal Blade over the years. Brian was, and is, a heavy metal hero to me.*

Was it always an ambition of yours to actually perform in a band? Was Metal Blade always receptive to the idea of *you* being signed to the label?
It's a funny story about how I got signed. I opened for one of Brian's bands, Charred Walls of the Damned, doing comedy. I have done lots of them since then, but this was my first tour doing something like that. Brian had come out to a few of the shows and dug what I was doing. He asked me if I would be interested in recording an album with him. I honestly thought he was fucking with me, so I never gave him an answer. Months later, he hired me to perform at an event he was organizing, and he reminded me that I never got back to him on doing an album for Metal Blade. When I realized he was serious, I said yes, and we had the deal done in his Prius in less than five minutes.

Richard Christy, who used to be in Death, Iced Earth, and a bunch of other bands, won a contest in 2004 that *The Howard Stern Show* was running to replace a long-serving member of the team, "Stuttering John" Melendez. I vaguely knew who Richard was, but had probably only met him for a minute when he was on the road somewhere with one of our bands. I had been a huge fan of Stern since the 1980s, so I thought it was kind of cool that a metal guy had found his way onto the show.

Over time, Richard and I became very good friends, and, by extension, I made friends with a few of the other staff members on Stern's show. As a result, we've had a few artists appear on the air over the years. One day I said to Richard, who was signed to Metal Blade with his band Charred Walls of the Damned by that point, "Hey, why don't you try to promote your record on the Stern show?" It made sense to me, since Stern's audience numbers something between five and seven million daily listeners on satellite radio. Then, after the main show, there's a follow-up called *The Wrap-Up Show*, which often showcases bands and their music.

A few years later, Richard said "Why don't you come on the show?" I said, "If they'd have me, I'd love to." They put me on, it went great, and hopefully I'll be able to do more things with them in the future. The whole experience was surreal. There I was, a massive fan since the 1980s, in the actual studio. It made no sense at all, but it was a massive amount of fun!

An Interview with Richard Christy

How did your interest in heavy music start?

I had a really cool aunt who was into KISS. When I was four years old, she gave me the KISS Alive album and the Peter Criss solo album. I remember just staring at the crowd picture on the back of the Alive album for hours. I was fascinated with the look of KISS and the fact that their fans would dress up, too. Then, when I was nine years old, a neighbor friend who was a few years older played me Quiet Riot's Metal Health album on cassette, and I was hooked. I've been a diehard metalhead ever since!

The following year, in 1984, I heard Van Halen's "Hot for Teacher," and I knew I had to be a drummer. It just so happened that was the same year my school offered band class, and I've been a drummer ever since. My neighbor friend always had the newest metal cassettes, like Twisted Sister's Stay Hungry and Iron Maiden's Live After Death. He would play them for me, and I would just be blown away. I'm so thankful that I had a neighbor who was a metalhead back in the 1980s! I feel fortunate that I discovered heavy metal in 1983, right when it was beginning to become a major force in music in the 1980s. If I was granted one wish, it would be to go back to the year 1986, when so many incredible albums came out. I was just twelve years old at the time, and looking back, I wish I would have realized what a legendary year that would become in heavy metal.

What was it that drew you to the drums?

I was instantly drawn to the drums when I was a kid because I grew up in Kansas, and there were always cow feed buckets and sticks around to bang on. I remember setting up five cow feed buckets in a circle to play along to "Cum on Feel the Noize" by Quiet Riot. The opening drum beat was easy to play, so I was so excited that I could actually come close to playing the drums on that song.

Then, as I mentioned, when I heard "Hot for Teacher" by Van Halen, I instantly wanted to try to figure out how to play the drum intro. I'm sorry to say I still haven't figured out how the hell to play it! It's one of the greatest drum intros of all time. The ride cymbal, the double bass—everything about the drumming in that song is perfect.

Hearing Metallica for the first time also changed my life—hearing how fast the drums on "Hit the Lights" were. I wanted to learn how to play that fast. At the time, the fastest songs I had ever heard were "Hit the Lights," "Fast as a Shark" by Accept, and "Ace of Spades" by Motörhead. Practicing drums to those songs helped build up my speed and made me want to try to be the fastest drummer I could.

My parents were so cool and supportive, too. When I was ten years old, they bought me a three-piece Gretsch drum set at a junk shop for a hundred dollars. It was tiny, but it was enough to try to play along to Metal Massacre *cassettes when I was a kid! I was so lucky that, when I was around ten years old, my family moved to a farm out in the middle of nowhere, so nobody ever complained about the drumming noise coming from my bedroom. My parents even used to take naps while I drummed in the next room. I don't know how they could do it, but somehow they were able to block out my noise!*

What was your first point of contact with Brian and Metal Blade?

I've been a fan of Brian's since I heard of him in the 1980s. He's a metal god! I used to order the Metal Massacre *cassettes from the Enigma Records catalog. I remember ordering Lizzy Borden cassettes from the Enigma catalog, too. I'm a big Lizzy Borden fan, especially the* Master of Disguise *album. I first met Brian by email because he contacted me to say that he was a listener of* The Howard Stern Show, *where I work. I remember thinking how amazing it was that Brian listened to the show.*

If I remember correctly, the first time I met him in person was July 16, 2006, at the Sounds of the Underground tour stop in the parking lot of the Starland Ballroom in Sayreville, New Jersey. I remember being really excited when I found out that Brian was a fan of Coheed and Cambria, because I'm a huge fan of theirs as well. We bonded over that right away.

Cannibal Corpse was on that tour, and we all ended up hanging out on the bus after their set. George "Corpsegrinder" Fisher and I are big fans of the German thrash metal band Rage, and every time we hang out, we blast their album Perfect Man—*specifically the song "Wasteland," which we sing along to at the top of our lungs! I'm sure we nearly blew out Brian Slagel's eardrums singing the high notes from "Wasteland" that day.*

Then, when I put Charred Walls of the Damned together in late 2008, the first person and label I thought about was Brian and Metal Blade. I'm a fan of so many bands on the label, and I knew Brian was such a down-to-earth and awesome guy. I sent him the Charred Walls of the Damned demos, and the rest is history!

Describe the background and evolution of Charred Walls of the Damned.

I moved from Florida to New York City in 2004 to join The Howard Stern Show. *I didn't have a band from 2004 through 2008, and I really missed playing music. I still practiced drums almost every day, but I also started practicing guitar a lot more when I moved to New York. Even though I didn't have a band for several years, I still wrote and recorded a lot of riffs when I would practice guitar.*

Around 2008, I realized I had enough riffs and rough blueprints of songs that I could put together an album. That's when I called up Tim Owens, Steve DiGiorgio, and Jason Suecof to see if they'd be interested in joining a group I was putting together. When they said yes, I was super excited, and I started working hard on putting really good demos together for an album. When I had a good set of songs, I sent them to Brian, and he really liked them. He offered us a deal with Metal Blade Records, and it was a dream come true!

When I was ordering Metal Massacre *cassettes through the mail at twelve years old, I could never have imagined that one day I would be making music that would be released on the same record label! Since Tim, Steve, Jason, and I had known each other for so long, and had played in other bands together, we instantly gelled. The music came together perfectly. You can hear influences from all our former bands in our music, but they also blend together to create something totally unique. The facility where we record, Audiohammer Studios in Sanford, Florida—which is Jason's studio—is the perfect place for us to record. I actually had a hand in helping Jason build it. I helped lay the wood flooring in the original drum room when I lived with him way back in 2000. I love recording there, and now that we're on our third album that's been recorded there, we have it down to a science. I think our most recent [third] album is our best-sounding one yet!*

How has the working relationship been with Metal Blade? What sets it apart from other labels in the business?

It has been amazing. I trust Brian's instincts so much because he's been involved in heavy metal for so long, and he's discovered so many legendary bands. I always ask him which songs from our albums he thinks would make good singles and videos, what order the songs should be in on the album, and things like that. Everybody at Metal Blade is so cool, and they're all genuine metalheads.

I've been to one of the Metal Blade Christmas parties in Los Angeles, and it was a blast. I wish I didn't live so far away, so I could go every year. I turn into a Metal Blade fanboy at their Christmas party, because I see such legendary metalheads like Joey Vera, Ray Adler, Lizzy Borden, and producer Bill Metoyer. Metal Blade treats their artists so great, and it doesn't even feel like a label as much as it feels like your friends who are also metalheads who are making sure your music gets out there to the masses. I'm so lucky to be a part of the family. They've done such an amazing job getting Charred Walls of the Damned's music out there to the people, and I'm so thankful for that. Because of Metal Blade, people are out there listening to my band, and hopefully banging their heads. Brian and Metal Blade absolutely rule!

Chapter 11
INTO THE FUTURE

Looking back on thirty-five years running Metal Blade, there are a few underlying themes that have pretty much underpinned everything we've done since 1982. One guiding principle I'm really proud of is that we have never been a label that anyone could look at and say, "Oh, Metal Blade signs *x* type of bands or *y* type of bands."

With the exception of what's known become known as nu-metal—which generally didn't sit well with me—we have been involved in almost every movement that has happened in heavy music since 1982. There's been no formula and no theorizing. It's simply been a longstanding policy that if we like something, we'll sign it. And that's how it will always be.

Obviously, an approach like that comes with its pitfalls. Over the years, we've had our share of records that haven't done well, or bands that have underachieved or been unlucky to be in the wrong place at the wrong time. But, in both cases, the way I look at it is that at least we tried to make a good record, and at least we gave these bands a chance. Nobody really loses. And, at a record label that's been around for three and a half decades, it's unrealistic to hope that you're going to hit the board with every dart you throw. That's not going to happen, but I'm a firm believer in the idea that, to be successful, you've *got* to keep throwing the darts.

William Berrol
Metal Blade's enduring strength is inextricably linked to Brian having this deep-seated passion for this kind of music. To my mind, he's probably the

world's foremost authority on it. I don't know anyone who knows more about heavy metal and hard rock music than he does. That combination of authority and wonderful taste—that's the Metal Blade DNA.

Another important principle is that we've continually sought to move with the times in terms of technology. Granted, we haven't always been at the point of the arrow of change. After all, a diehard like me is going to be a little resistant sometimes (as illustrated by my reluctance to flush vinyl in the late 1980s), but Metal Blade has always made changes when necessary. We've been open to new partnerships, alliances, and ideas, all in the spirit of selling records and championing the heavy metal genre.

Finally, I'd like to think we really do run the business, and specifically the artist roster, like a family. Without the artists, nothing happens. As I've said before, they don't work for Metal Blade; Metal Blade works for them. The fact that several bands have remained with us for their whole careers, despite offers from much bigger labels, is a testament to how we try to treat everybody. Like all families, it's not always a bed of roses. There are disagreements and misunderstandings, but my policy—and that of the Metal Blade staff—is to find a solution, move on, and keep the ball rolling. That's how it'll always be.

John Bush

Although we're pretty close in age, Brian is like a father figure to me. He's been supportive of the majority of things we've done, but he certainly has no problem telling us things he doesn't like or what he'd prefer us to do as the label boss. That's his job. And I always say that, without Brian, there is no Armored Saint.

Chris Barnes

I'm lucky enough to have had Metal Blade as a home for twenty-eight years, good and bad. And I say that because I haven't exactly been an angel over the years. I've been kind of a pain in the ass. But I've always tried to make Brian proud of me and to impress him, because he's been like a big brother to me.

But where is the record business going?

We're definitely moving from the physical to the streaming business. What it looks like is happening is that, by 2020, the streaming business will be ten times its current size. Digital downloads will be gone within two to five years. In fact, the companies that currently offer downloads actually *want* people to move to the streaming services.

In 2017, there are roughly 50 million subscribers to streaming services. If the estimates of industry experts are correct, that number will be five *hundred* million in just three years. Clearly the way people—especially young people—are consuming their entertainment is moving toward streaming. Consumers are increasingly skipping cable TV and streaming on Apple TV, Roku, or whatever instead. Music is no different; it's changing faster than I've ever seen it change before, and that's from someone who's been in the midst of it all for thirty-five years. I've seen a lot of change, but never like this.

This groundswell applies only to certain parts of the world. Germany, for example, is resistant to the change, particularly in the metal world. Even when metal was seemingly dead in the nineties, and *Rock Hard* put that tombstone on their front cover, it was still *less* dead in Germany than anywhere else! Unbelievably, the physical product still accounts for 80 percent of the total metal market there. They still buy physical magazines, and high-speed internet is not as readily available in Germany as you'd think. The attitude is, "This is the way we've always done it, so this is the way we'll keep doing it." The same applies to France, Switzerland, and the Benelux countries.

On the flip side, you have a country like Sweden, where the physical market is almost non-existent. Spotify completely took over. And North America is moving in that direction—particularly given that high speed internet will probably be available to everybody, either free or at minimal cost, by 2020. Everyone will have access.

Of course, the argument I always hear against this change is, "What if I'm on a remote island somewhere and want to listen to my music? Without being able to access a computer or have it downloaded on my phone, I can't do it." Well, from what I'm told, with the speed at which satellites are being launched, there'll be high speed internet pretty much everywhere. Wherever you are, you *will* have access.

The arguments the other way are pretty compelling, too. I hear kids who have student rates on Spotify say things like, "I have every song ever recorded on my phone for $5.99 a month. Why would I ever want to buy a record?" As hard as it is to admit for someone who's been so entrenched in the record business, it's a fair point. When I was a kid, $5.99 bought *one* record!

What's happening is a move away from the concept of music ownership and towards the concept of music *access*. That said, it's not going to be the case that streaming will be the only way people can consume music. Fans are always going to want to buy tangible products that you can hold in your hand. But the CD is going to become what vinyl is now: a specialty item that people will still want to buy, particularly in certain countries and particularly among older buyers.

※

So, what does it all mean for the *next* thirty-five years of a record label like Metal Blade? If the projected numbers hold up, artists and labels are going to be making more money on that side of the music than they have in a long time. There's a bright future there for artists and the music business in general. We just have to get there.

As it stands, we're seeing a huge drop-off in our existing market. We knew this was going to happen and, for a while, it had been a slow and steady process. But now, with major retail outlets in the United States barely carrying CDs any longer (and only a few hundred independent stores carrying them), it's no surprise that this market swing is really starting to bite. From my perspective, all

I can say is, "Why not? Go sign up with a streaming service and, for ten bucks a month, you can listen to all our stuff!"

The question people ask most often is, "How does anyone make money from streaming?" Previously, with vinyl, CDs, cassette tapes, and, to a lesser extent, digital downloads, there was a physical product to which a value was attached. And then, when it was sold, the artist and the label, among others, were paid a percentage of that sale, but there was obviously an initial cost to manufacture and market that physical product.

With streaming services, every time a song is streamed or played, that activity is tracked. The more streams there are, the more you get paid. In 2016, Metal Blade's streaming income started getting to a level I'd call "quite high." And it's getting higher every month—to the extent that there have been months in the US market where our streaming income has exceeded our physical income. Obviously that has never happened before now, and it's beginning to look like real money.

Like the vinyl to CD shift back in the late eighties, the transition might be a little difficult. Having experienced the pitfalls firsthand back in 1989, Metal Blade will have to be careful how we move along. The streaming hasn't yet consistently made up for the loss of physical purchases. A deficit still exists, but experts are predicting that within a year or less, everything should even itself out.

Moving forward, the nature of what we exist to do will change. In the early days, a big part of our role was to pay for recording costs, and then we had to spend a lot of money manufacturing products to put into stores. To a certain degree, we'll still have to do that, but it will be much less extensive than it was. The risk that we'll have to bear as a record company will be much less than it once was because we're not fronting the same manufacturing costs we once did. If we do manufacture anything, we'll be doing so with a pretty good understanding of what we're likely to sell.

Without sounding too corporate, I can see Metal Blade moving away from that traditional record company role and toward a new identity as a *brand-building company*. As such, our resources—what we do and the people we have working for us—will be deployed in a completely new way. Instead of making records and CDs, we'll be promoting brands, and the brands are our artists themselves.

Our job (along with the agents and managers) will be to pump up the artists as much as humanly possible and to make the brand as big as it can possibly be, in the hope that everything else will come together. Our role will be more like a service company than a traditional record label. That's where the smart labels are going—partnering with artists and helping them achieve their goals from multiple angles: selling out concerts, selling tons of t-shirts, and, in turn, getting people who go to the shows to stream the music.

There are so many different income sources now that were inconceivable back in the days when I was working around the clock out of my mom's garage. We have staff dedicated to plowing through them—figuring out income from downloading, streaming, physical CD sales, vinyl sales, and everything else.

In many ways, this new direction will fit well with the family ethos that Metal Blade has always fostered. Since 1982, we've always felt that we're partners with our artists, so it'll be no different from that perspective.

Regardless of any changes in the way music is consumed and sold, Metal Blade will continue to do the fundamental function that has been the absolute core of the label since we started: finding and investing in new heavy metal acts. The desire to identify the next Slayer or the next Amon Amarth is still what drives me.

New bands are the lifeblood of not only Metal Blade, but of heavy metal in general. That's the primary reason I got into any of this. The difference is that it's now ten times harder to break an artist and to make something happen for them. It can be a five- to ten-year cycle from when you sign a band to when something develops. That's a lot of time, a lot of money, and a lot of effort.

I often hear people say, "There will never be another Metallica," but you never know. Part of the challenge is that older bands like Metallica are still performing at an extremely high level. People still love going to see them, and they're still amazing. I saw them play recently at Webster Hall, a small 2,000-seat venue in New York City. I've seen them play maybe two hundred times since Lars Ulrich handed me that demo cassette for *Metal Massacre*, in all kinds of different venues over the years. But this was the first time I'd seen them somewhere I'd seen tons of other shows. They are, hands down, better than any other metal band out there. Given the way in which our lives and careers have been intertwined over these thirty-five years, it was amazing to see how phenomenal they still are. They've set the bar so incredibly high. In 1982, none of us, in a million years, ever would have imagined that what we were doing at the time would become as huge as it is. That was unfathomable, so I can't sit here and tell you something like that will never happen again. You just never can tell. And that's been the most exciting part of this thirty-five-year joyride. I can't wait to see what's down the line.

SELECTED INTERVIEWEES' TOP METAL BLADE ALBUM PICKS

Richard Christy
Mercyful Fate—*In the Shadows*
Banshee Night—*Cry in the Night*
Amon Amarth—*With Oden on Our Side*
Ignorance—*The Confidence Rat*
Cannibal Corpse—*Tomb of the Mutilated*

Johan Hegg
Slayer—*Hell Awaits*
Bolt Thrower—*Honour, Valour, Pride*
Vomitory—*Carnage Euphoria*
Primordial—*The Gathering Wilderness*
The Crown—*Hell Is Here*

Joey Vera
Kings X—*Tapehead*
Gwar—*Scumdogs of the Universe*
OSI—*Office of Strategic Influence*
3—*Wakepig*
Screw—*Burning in Water, Drowning in Flame*

John Bush
Gwar—*Scumdogs of the Universe*
Engine—*Engine*
Sacred Reich—*Surf Nicaragua*

Mike Faley
Cannibal Corpse—*Kill*
As I Lay Dying—*Frail Words Collapse*
Unearth—*The Oncoming Storm*
Armored Saint—*Symbol of Salvation*
The Black Dahlia Murder—*Unhallowed*
In Solitude—*Sister*

Tracy Vera
Armored Saint—*Symbol of Salvation*
Fates Warning—*A Pleasant Shade of Gray*
Goo Goo Dolls—*Hold Me Up*
Thin Lizzy—*Thunder and Lightning (Reissue)*
Motor Sister—*Ride*

Tracy Vera (handicap list—minus her husband)
Goo Goo Dolls—*Hold Me Up*
Amon Amarth—*Twilight of the Thundergods*
Fates Warning—*Parallels*
Kings X—*Tapehead*
Flotsam and Jetsam—*Doomsday for the Deceiver*

Alex Webster
Cryptic Slaughter—*Money Talks*
Slayer—*Haunting the Chapel (EP)*
Hallows Eve—*Monument*
Aeon—*Path of Fire*
Sacrifice—*Forward to Termination*

Brad Roberts

Corrosion of Conformity—*Animosity*
DRI—*Four of a Kind*
Cancer Bat—*Searching for Zero*
Battle Cross—*Rise to Power*
Trouble—*Run to the Light*

Bill Metoyer

Trouble—*The Skull*
Flotsam and Jetsam—*Doomsday for the Deceiver*
Fates Warning—*Awaken the Guardian*
Slayer—*Hell Awaits*
Slayer—*Show No Mercy*

Don Jamieson

Amon Amarth—*Jomsviking*
King Diamond—*Give Me Your Soul… Please*
Armored Saint—*Win Hands Down*
Slayer—*Hell Awaits*
Six Feet Under—*Commandment*

William Berrol

Various Artists—*Metal Massacre* (the beginning of it all)
Fates Warning—*Perfect Symmetry*
Slayer—*Hell Awaits* (music to kill your parents to)
Princess Pang—*Trouble in Paradise*
Goo Goo Dolls—*Hold Me Up*

Betsy Weiss

Cirith Ungol—*Frost and Fire*
Riot—*Fire Down Under*
Various Artists—*Metal Massacre*
Armored Saint—*March of the Saint*
Y&T—*Y&T Live*

Chris Barnes
Slayer—*Show No Mercy*
Slayer—*Haunting the Chapel*
Warlord—*Deliver Us*
Witchkiller—*March of the Saxons*
Trouble—*Psalm 9*

Lizzy Borden
Alice Cooper—*Muscle of Love (Reissue)*
Deep Purple—*Come Taste the Band (Reissue)*
Alice Cooper—*From the Inside (Reissue)*
Deep Purple—*Live in Europe (Reissue)*
Thin Lizzy—*Thunder and Lightning (Reissue)*

ACKNOWLEDGMENTS

Thanks to my mom, my family, Tracy Vera, Bill Berrol, Mike Faley, Vince Edwards, Heather Parsons, Matthew Taylor, Dan Fitzgerald, Brian Ames, Nikki Law, Andreas, Will, Andy, Bart, Armin, and the entire amazing Metal Blade family, past and present.

Also all the incredible artists, managers, agents, retailers, radio, press, and everyone I have had the pleasure to work with over the years.

Scott, Emi, and Kate from BMG; Mark Eglinton, and everyone who helped out with this project; Lars Ulrich for the incredible words at the beginning of the book and the years of friendship.

All my friends for helping fuel so many great stories, many of which are in this book!

Finally, all the fans out there: if not for you, we would not exist!

Heavy metal will never die!